UNQUENCHED

UNQUENCHED

In Pursuit of the Supernatural

JONATHAN *and* AMANDA
FERGUSON

Foreword by Apostle Guillermo Maldonado

New York   Nashville

FaithWords
Hachette Book Group
1290 Avenue of the Americas, New York, NY 10104
faithwords.com
twitter.com/faithwords

First Edition: October 2019

FaithWords is a division of Hachette Book Group, Inc. The FaithWords name and logo
are trademarks of Hachette Book Group, Inc.

The publisher is not responsible for websites (or their content) that are not owned by the
publisher.

Unless otherwise noted, Scripture quotations are taken from the King James Version of
the Bible. Public domain. | Scripture quotations marked NKJV are taken from the New
King James Version®. Copyright © 1982 by Thomas Nelson. Used by permission. All
rights reserved. | Scripture quotations marked NIV are taken from the Holy Bible, New
International Version®, NIV®. Copyright ©1973, 1978, 1984, 2011 by Biblica,
Inc.™ Used by permission of Zondervan. All rights reserved worldwide.
www.zondervan.com. The "NIV" and "New International Version" are trademarks
registered in the United States Patent and Trademark Office by Biblica, Inc.™

Library of Congress Cataloging-in-Publication Data
Names: Ferguson, Jonathan, author.
Title: Unquenched : in pursuit of the supernatural / Jonathan and Amanda Ferguson ;
foreword by Apostle Guillermo Maldonado. Description: First [edition]. | New York :
Faith Words, 2019. Identifiers: LCCN 2019019050 | ISBN 9781546035848 (trade
pbk.) | ISBN 9781546035831 (ebook) Subjects: LCSH: Spirituality—Christianity. |
Spiritual life—Christianity. | Supernatural. Classification: LCC BV4501.3 .F4667 2019
| DDC 248.4—dc23. LC record available at https://lccn.loc.gov/2019019050 ISBNs:
978-1-5460-3584-8 (trade paperback), 978-1-5460-3583-1 (ebook)

Printed in the United States of America

LSC-C

10 9 8 7 6 5 4 3 2 1

TABLE OF CONTENTS

TABLE OF CONTENTS

FOREWORD

There is the supernatural divine and the supernatural demonic. If the Church does not understand the supernatural, or is afraid of it, we will be at a disadvantage against the power of ignorance, fear, and deception. Further, we will miss out on the fullness of the abundant life that Jesus promised us (John 10:10).

For over twenty-five years, I have taught the importance of standing in the full counsel of God in this and every other matter. We must understand that God is supernatural and that we have been given authority over the power of the devil though Christ Jesus (Luke 10:19). Particularly so in these End Times, where there is an increase of demonic activity, we simply cannot teach the Bible without also teaching on the supernatural power of God so clearly evident from Genesis to Revelation, nor can we go to the dangerous extreme of teaching or engaging in the supernatural in any way without the Word of God and the guidance of the Holy Spirit.

I am deeply thankful to others in the Body of Christ who also proclaim these important truths, including my spiritual children: Apostle Jonathan and Prophet Amanda Ferguson.

Unquenched is an important book that I recommend all believers to read. Apostle Jonathan and Prophet Amanda have teamed up to write this new book, and have done an excellent job of bringing revelation to the reality that we must know how to engage the supernatural realm in the name of Jesus, as we are facing a very real war, not against flesh and blood, but against demonic principalities, powers, and rulers of darkness (Ephesians 6:12) that seek to kill, steal, and destroy us physically, emotionally, mentally, and ultimately spiritually (John 10:10). We must recognize the tactics of the supernatural demonic and know how to fight against it.

More important, I recommend *Unquenched* because it leads the reader to recognizing the Word of God as the eternal, unchanging truth and the Holy Spirit as our only guide concerning the supernatural divine and its many benefits: salvation, healing, deliverance, prosperity, and more that Jesus purchased for us through His death on the cross and resurrection. God alone, through His Spirit, can reveal the knowledge of the glory that will cover the earth (Habakkuk 2:14), as we seek out the Scriptures and the manifestation of His presence and power.

Unquenched will empower the reader to understand that only God can lead us to the awesome benefits of the supernatural divine and protect us from the evils of the supernatural demonic.

Apostle Guillermo Maldonado
King Jesus Ministry
Miami, Florida

INTRODUCTION

OPENING YOUR EYES

JONATHAN'S VISION

In a vision, I saw what looked like a world gathering that would be comparable to a city or county fair. At this gathering, every religion you could imagine was there. Governments were represented, every form of dark arts and witchcraft was there, and Christians too. I knew through the Spirit that this attempt was to bring about some type of unity among religions in a way that would set the world up for an anti-Christ agenda.

At this world gathering, I also noticed that every religion and every type of witchcraft was accepted. The only people who were not accepted were Spirit-filled Christians. We were the outcasts of the event. I saw myself leading a group of millennial Christians around the fair, and I noticed that we became the focus of people's mockery or disgust.

Next, various occultists, demonic priests, warlocks,

voodoo workers, and every other type of witchcraft began gathering around the Spirit-filled Christians to challenge us. As I began to step back and look, I noticed that the Christians' "defense statement" to the occultists was, "We don't believe in that." I also noticed that these Christians were very confident and felt that just because they didn't subscribe to those practices, they were safe.

The witches and warlocks then began to challenge their stance by practicing magic on them. I watched as witches began to cast spells on Christians, who were then falling to the floor and responding much like it would look in a Spirit-filled service if they were reacting to the power of God coming on them. The only difference was that they were visibly in torment and they were screaming from the pain.

At that moment, something rose in me. I stepped forward and I said, "What you're doing is real. God talks about your power all throughout His book." When I said this, they stopped casting spells on the Christians and gathered around me, supposing they had found a place of unity. Not only did the witches lend me their attention, but the government and the other religions began to pay attention as they huddled around me.

I began to walk them through the Scriptures of the Bible, from Genesis to Revelation, and showed them the reality of demonic powers. After this, I then looked at them and said, "See, your power is real. But the only problem is, the supreme power is in the name of Jesus."

When I said that, the witches and warlocks began to

fall on the floor, overtaken by the power of God, and demons began to scream as they came out of many of them.

After this, I came out of the vision.

That encounter shook me to my core, and called me to pursue an understanding of the supernatural scripturally as I never had before. There are a couple of things that I took from it. The Spirit of the Lord began to speak to me about what was coming. The Lord also began to show me that we are at a disadvantage to what is coming, although we are Spirit-filled Christians, because we lack understanding of the supernatural. He showed me that if we don't begin to educate ourselves about spiritual things, we're not going to be ready for what's coming. This is when He anointed me to write this book.

God has taken me through multiple supernatural experiences, which you'll read about in *Unquenched*. Not only that, but He's shown me through the Scriptures how to understand these experiences biblically, something that has been lacking in the Church. We either teach the supernatural without proper scriptural foundation or we teach the Scripture without any supernatural dealings.

This book is a solution to this problem.

In addition to this, my wife had an experience that altered the trajectory of her childhood. I believe it was the beginning, equipping her later in life to be ready to contribute to this book. Her encounter was not pleasant. However, what the enemy meant for evil, God turned it around for Amanda's good.

AMANDA'S ENCOUNTER

A lady, I'll call her Kelly, came to our house one day for prayer. My mom told her that she could come into her bedroom while she finished up a phone call.

As my mom was ending her phone call, Kelly began to glare at her. Then, before my mom could hang up the phone, Kelly started to speak. Out of Kelly's mouth came these words, "She's so sanctified she deserves to die."

My mom responded, "No, she doesn't."

Kelly responded, "Yes, she does."

My mom responded, "No, she doesn't, in the name of Jesus."

Kelly then fell on the floor and began to scream as if she were in complete torment. I have never heard a scream so shrill. Even more than twenty years later, I can still remember how terrible the sound of her screaming was.

I was in my bedroom during the ordeal, but as soon as I heard the bloodcurdling screaming, I ran out of my room to stand in front of my mother's room.

As I stood at her door, I saw that Kelly was now in a fetal position on the floor. Her body was gyrating and twisting while she was screaming.

I stood in the hallway and began to cry. My mother asked my brother to grab me and take me into another room while she prayed over the lady.

My mom asked the lady, "Who are you?"

Kelly responded, "LEGIONS!"

Of course, now I know that it wasn't her, but thousands upon thousands of demons crying out from inside her. From my small, innocent vantage point, I couldn't understand how the sweet lady from church transformed into this person on my mother's floor.

I was literally shaking. And though I was in my mother's doorway for only a few minutes before my brother scooped me up, it was enough to truly impact me. I was so afraid. I didn't understand what was going on at the time, but that experience shut me off to the supernatural because I was so afraid of spiritual things. Honestly, it was a terrible sight for a small girl. I don't remember my exact age, but I believe I was around ten years old.

My spiritual father, Apostle Maldonado, says it best: "There is a supernatural divine and there is a supernatural demonic."

Many of you reading this have had experiences and seen things in the demonic realm that have frightened you and made you frightened to be exposed to the supernatural divine.

I get it, and from that experience, I spent many months in mental, spiritual, and physical torment. I sat in my room so very afraid. I couldn't be in a room alone. My body was covered in hives, and the thought of anyone leaving me alone terrified me. I was just a little girl who had witnessed the most horrific scene of her life.

I'd always had beautiful, long hair. But due to so

much fear and fright, my entire nervous system was affected, and my hair began coming out in handfuls. I would sit and cry as my mother would do my hair, watching it fall to the floor in clumps.

It was also the beginning of severe skin issues. I had to go to the dermatologist for treatment because my body was attacked with hives, eczema, pimples, and all other types of skin issues.

Over the next two years I was still in fear and torment, I was bullied, and I was even sexually abused by my youth pastor.

From that point on, every time I was in the dark, I was afraid. Every time I was left alone, I was afraid. Every time I closed my eyes, I couldn't stop seeing images of that day. I would cry and have nightmares in my sleep. It weighed down my entire family. This went on for *months*.

I was grasped by the spirit of fear. Fear is *torment*. Many of you reading this have had experiences with the spirit of fear, and some may even be dealing with it now. Though I was delivered from it in time, I still had to go through deliverance from it as an adult.

The year before I got married, my mother passed away. After I got married, I would be afraid for my husband to go to the store at night. What if something happened to him? A series of other events happened that year that made me believe the lies of the enemy: everything I loved would be taken away.

Here are some manifestations of the spirit of fear:

Always feeling like something bad will happen
Always feeling anxious or dealing with anxiety
Feeling unusually timid

There is much more that I can discuss about this tormenting spirit, but I don't have time to delve into an
in-depth teaching because it's not the focus of this book.
But remember, God has not given us the spirit of fear
but of love and of power and clarity of mind!

One moment in the presence of God, and fear can be
gone for a lifetime. The thoughts may come to test you
at times, but you do not have to live in torment. This
is my prayer for you as you read. Through this book, I
believe you will experience freedom from fear of spiritual things. I'm confident that you will be okay as we
keep moving along so that you can better understand my
track record in supernatural realities.

As a little girl, I could smell demons. I remember being in a church service where demons were being cast
out of a lady. I caught the scent of the demons that had
been cast out of her as they went by me upon their exit.
The smell is hard to put into words. It was so terrible.
It smelled like sulfur, but more horrific than that. Even
in that moment, I began to cry, because at a young age,
I couldn't explain how overwhelmed I felt by being able
to smell those demons and experience such senses in the
supernatural.

Likewise, many people are afraid of the *supernatural
divine*, because of their experiences with the supernatural

demonic. Maybe this is you. It was me. But I want to let you know that you do not need to be afraid.

Let me say a prayer over you now:

Father God, in the name of Jesus, I ask You to bless the person reading this. Deliver them from the spirit of fear and every tormenting spirit that would try to hinder them from experiencing the divine part of the supernatural. I ask for You to heal every part of them that is hurting.

It was a rough time. But I came to see the truth that all things work together for the good of those who are called according to His purpose!

A WAKE-UP CALL

Like Amanda, I've learned through many years of experience that just because we believers are not engaging the supernatural dimension does not mean that the demons decide to take a break. If we are not engaging the spiritual dimension, I can guarantee you that witches and warlocks are. What's worse is that if we do not understand the supernatural dimension, we cannot expect to engage it. This leaves a void and a vacancy in the Spirit that can potentially cause a breach.

God is seeking to fill the gap (Ezekiel 22:30) in our spiritual understanding. We are living in days much like 1 Samuel 3:1, where there is a lack vision of spiritual insight, and the days of Amos 8:11, where there is a famine for the Word of God. This is what Jesus Himself faced in John 3 with Nicodemus, who was a respected religious leader. Jesus was shocked that Nicodemus was a spiritual leader of that day, but could not understand the spiritual things that Jesus was trying to communicate with him.

But there is good news! We have a promise from God that we are not going to continue down the wrong path. Habakkuk 2:14 promises that there is going to be a continuous growing demand for the knowledge of the glory of God. There is a remnant of people who are in pursuit of the supernatural, and that remnant will become the majority soon enough.

If you have been wondering if there is more, I want you to know there is. Read this book as a wake-up call, and allow my wife and me to take you on a journey that will awaken you and cause you to know and serve God at your maximum capacity. We want to experience all we can experience in God, be all He has called us to be, do all He has called us to do, and show the world His supernatural power. Join us on this incredible journey!

CHAPTER 1

THERE IS MORE: KNOWING THE WAYS AND ACTS OF GOD

The Knowledge of the Glory will cover the earth as the waters the sea.

Habakkuk 2:14 (paraphrased)

As we get closer to the return of Jesus Christ, we are going to see and experience what the Bible mentions in Habakkuk 2:14. But Habakkuk 2:14 is teaching something deeper too. The glory of God has its own archive of knowledge that must be released by God Himself. We can only understand what that knowledge is by studying the Scriptures and allowing the Spirit to bring us into an experience of what we're reading. We need the Holy Spirit's help to understand more fully.

Jesus tells us this in John 5:39–45 (NIV):

"You study the Scriptures diligently because you think that in them you have eternal life. These are the very Scriptures that testify about me, yet you refuse to come to me to have life.

"I do not accept glory from human beings, but I know you. I know that you do not have the love of God in your hearts. I have come in my Father's name, and you do not accept me; but if someone else comes in his own name, you will accept him. How can you believe since you accept glory from one another but do not seek the glory that comes from the only God?"

Jesus was explaining that the religious leaders of His time really didn't know the Scriptures the way they thought they did. He instructed them to "search the Scriptures," which meant to undergo a thorough investigation. Next, Jesus informed them as to *why* their study of Scripture needed a more thorough investigation. Because they refused to come to Jesus, they weren't experiencing the one person who the entire Scriptures are about.

We don't want to refuse Jesus the way that the religious leaders did in John 5:39. Therefore, you should understand that this book you're holding in your hands is not merely to help you learn more about the supernatural. I'm sure you will learn a lot in the process.

We are going to thoroughly examine the Scriptures concerning the supernatural, and you are going to begin experiencing what you have learned. But this is about a lot more than head knowledge. It's about experiencing

Jesus by the end, and delving into the supernatural in ways you never have before. This is the proper way to pursue the knowledge of spiritual things.

THE SIGNIFICANCE OF THE GLORY OF GOD

If there was one word, other than the word *supernatural*, to explain spiritual things, that word would be "glory." The glory of God is significant because it ties the importance of the supernatural to a prophetic promise from Scripture: the prophetic promise of the supernatural glory of God expanding throughout the entire world, found in Habakkuk 2:14. And if the knowledge of the glory is going to cover the earth like the waters cover the sea, it must mean that the knowledge of the glory cannot be exhausted. Its knowledge is vast.

I don't think there is one book that can explain God's glory, because it's never ending. In light of that, we are going to cover various dynamics of many spiritual realities in the context of the supernatural world. But I'm not going to pretend to try to communicate everything that can be understood of the glory of God. No book can. The Bible didn't even try.

But to put it simply, the glory doesn't have one particular emphasis other than God Himself, and everything He represents. The glory is not an encounter we have at a prophetic conference. The glory of God is found only in the person of Jesus Christ (2 Corinthians 4:6).

The first time the word *glory* was mentioned in Scripture, it represented wealth. At other times, the *shekinah* glory represented the physical and visible manifestation of God, while the *kabad* or *kabod* represented the heavy weight and tangibility of God's manifest presence that is often associated with His appearance. In addition to this, glory has represented strength, and it has also represented honor in the Scripture. I think you get the point. Glory is dimensional. There are so many dynamics of the Spirit of God we explore when dealing with the glory.

From that archive of knowledge, my wife and I will focus predominately on the realities of the supernatural world, supernatural encounters, the Spirit-filled life, the power of God, and our divine nature.

There will always be a demand for the supernatural here on earth because of this reality of the prophecy given to us in Habakkuk 2:14. Even now there's a growing hunger and awareness of spiritual things. This is because God wants to show us something. He wants us to know more about who He is, more about His world, more about His power, and more about who He created us to be. This book serves to assist us in the process of understanding the vastness of what it means to really know God and walk with Him daily.

UNDERSTANDING SPIRITUAL DYNAMICS AND SUPERNATURAL REALITIES

It's one thing to have a passion to pursue the supernatural and the glory of God, but it's another thing to understand it. The fact that there's a knowledge of the glory that is going to blanket the earth means that the comprehension of spiritual dynamics will be widespread. Therefore, understanding spiritual dynamics is one goal of this book.

The spirit world is highly complex and we tend to overgeneralize or group spiritual things together that are intrinsically distinguished. We do this in an attempt to simplify the matter. We often assume that spiritual teaching is "too deep" for the average person. This couldn't be further from the truth. The supernatural can be easily understood if properly dissected. However, it is only easily explained by someone who has deeply experienced it.

Understanding the glory of God, the spirit realm, or the supernatural world is like having the mind of a mechanic, a brain surgeon, a therapist, a scientist, and a musician simultaneously. None of those experts in their field could ever grasp their work fully without extensive study and experience. In the same way, a person who is going to understand and operate in the glory of God must be completely devoted to it just as someone who is completely given to their craft.

Apostle Paul, in 1 Corinthians 12, urges us not to be

ignorant of spiritual things and of the supernatural, because God wants us to grow up in the maturity of the Word and in the maturity of the Spirit. He has also given us specialists in certain areas with certain abilities and gifts, so we can better understand and be groomed to operate in God's supernatural world.

TWO IMPORTANT LESSONS OF UNDERSTANDING SPIRITUAL DYNAMICS

As you begin to learn about spiritual things, one truth that will accelerate your learning is understanding that there is a difference between the person and the power of God. The person is who God is. The power is what He can do. The Scriptures mention the difference between the two in Psalm 103:7: Moses knew His ways and Israel His acts (paraphrased).

The *ways* of God are about the makeup of God's person. How do we know? Because Moses asked God to teach him His ways and show him His glory. When God did this, He showed Moses His name and His nature.

The *acts* of God are different. They are in reference to His power and His great signs and wonders.

Most people attempt to relate to God only through external means because they have not been taught that we can know God in a deeper way. What I mean by this is that their only relationship with God is in thinking about going to heaven, getting their needs met, asking him to rescue them out of danger, and helping them throughout life.

Our relationship with God can and should be more meaningful. We can know His personality, we can know His friendship, we can know His voice, we can know His heart, and we've even been invited to know and understand His world, which is the supernatural world. This understanding is key in having a healthy, right relationship with God. Often when people approach the supernatural, they do so from just one side: They embrace either the side of the supernatural in which they encounter and experience God, or the side of the supernatural in which they see the power of God. The reality is that a healthy relationship with God embraces more than these two spectrums.

Yes, God wants us to encounter Him in the supernatural and begin to understand the mysteries of His invisible world. He also wants us to demonstrate His power. But the most important thing is that we become like Him, transformed into His likeness. Transformation is key. When we are transformed, His ways become our ways. Second Corinthians 3:18 says we are changed into His image. Romans 8 teaches that those who are led by God's Spirit are the very offspring of God; and according to 2 Peter 1:4, it means we literally take on God's nature. This is the level that Enoch walked in before he was "no more" (Genesis 5:24). Enoch was so supernatural that he lived and walked in two worlds at the same time. He was human enough to walk on the earth, but spiritual enough to access heaven and walk with God at the same time.

Most important, before I close this chapter, I want to show you an encounter my wife had with Jesus Himself, in which He showed Himself to her in a vision and had a conversation with her about the supernatural. I believe it will keep your focus on what the priority of this pursuit in the supernatural is. It will also help inform you as to why you should seek a pure heart in your pursuit of spiritual things.

Amanda's Encounter with Jesus

I have had many stirring encounters with the Lord, but this one still shakes me to my core. Even now at this writing, I still feel the holiness and presence of it though it was years ago. It was a Sunday one summer in the month of June, and I felt pulled into prayer. At the most random times, I often feel a pull to pray, and I've learned how to yield to that pulling.

My husband was out of town, and our children were with the babysitter for a few hours, so I was excited to have a little alone time in prayer. I went into my room and turned on worship music. Then I began to pray and sing and worship the Lord. The more I prayed, the more I began to feel His presence. When I feel pulled into prayer, I don't always know what to expect, but I'm always in expectation of whatever the Lord wants to do or say.

I was playing one of my husband's albums, when the Lord spoke to me that He was about to come into our room. I felt as if our room was there, but not there, and all of a sudden I began to feel an overwhelming sense of God's presence, love, majesty, dominion...

It felt like there were a million people in the room with me, and I knew that it was the presence of angels. Words fail me to describe everything that I was feeling.

Then He began to speak to me and said:

Daughter, many people that I have chosen have gone astray. Many strong prophets and apostles that I've raised up have veered into a spirit of divination. They have prayed to go into a deeper place, but they haven't prayed to go into a deep level of repentance ALONG with closing the door that led to sin. Therefore, they've opened themselves up to another spirit. Many ask for forgiveness with no intention to close doors of sin. Many of them have fallen into traps of pride, love of money, and perversion. And so, they have gone deeper. Yet they haven't gone deeper in ME. They have gone deeper into a familiar spirit. Tell my people to posture themselves for repentance and shutting of doors to anything that isn't holy! Then and only then will they ascend into the high places of glory! If not, they will become workers of witchcraft although they are preachers in the pulpit.

It was then, in that moment, that I realized that if you seek *power* over *purity*, you will enter into witchcraft.

At this point, I began to weep. I felt the Lord's enormous

love so strong for people who had gone astray. At the same time, I felt the seriousness and holiness of the moment. I was completely overwhelmed.

But it didn't stop there. While I listened to a song called "Jesus Encounter," Jesus then let me know that He would come and visit me. I continued in worship, and He spoke to me to go to a particular part of the room and lift up my hands so that He could touch me. Once I did, I felt a weight so heavy that I fell down as if someone had knocked me down with a boulder. My knees buckled instantly, and it was hard to stand up and regain my balance.

The weight of His glory was indescribable!

Isn't that amazing! You'll hear more encounters from my wife as we go. However, as we briefly dig into this further, you will begin to understand more and more what I'm saying now about the knowledge of the glory. It's all about knowing Jesus and pursuing Him. For example, what attracted me to my wife was not her makeup and jewelry. Why? Because those are just her accessories. That's how the power of God is. It's just God's accessories.

Many want the power of God, but they do not want God. This is why it was important to set the tone in this chapter and be sure we all understand that our focus is Jesus and knowing Him. Everything in the supernatural comes along with knowing by default simply because He is supernatural. In fact, Jesus is the supernatural and He is who we are in pursuit of.

CHAPTER 2

THE SUPERNATURAL, IN THE BIBLE BUT OVERLOOKED

I, Amanda, remember the day like it was yesterday: May 16, 2009, at 3:00 a.m. It was a day that my life changed forever. It's the day that Jesus visited me face-to-face. I was on day one of three days of a full, water-only fast. At that time, I had been in a season of fasting for three consecutive days each month, combined with intense prayer, and studying of the Word. I was so desperate for more of the Lord. I had been saved for only a year and a half, but I had an insatiable desire to see Jesus and experience Him in a new way. Being closer to Him was all I thought about. He was my only desire!

This is what God wants. He wants us to desire only Him. The problem is you cannot desire what you have not been exposed to. The good news is *Unquenched* is the solution to that problem. Through this book we want to expose you to the supernatural divine. In doing so, it will put you on the right path to begin cultivating a passion-ate and fiery pursuit of the things of God. Furthermore, Scripture is very clear that this is what God desires for us believers to develop.

In 1 Thessalonians 5:19, we are admonished to live unquenched. The word *quench*, from its Greek origin, carries the connotation of putting out a fire. It's quite different from our English understanding of quenching thirst. God never wants the fiery passion of our pursuit of Him to die out.

When we are exposed to the supernatural, it lights a fire in our world. Our job is to ensure that fire is not quenched. The only way to keep a fire burning is to feed it. This is where pursuit comes into play. Scripture ac-tually teaches about fervent prayer in James 5:16. This is key, because the word *fervent* in the Greek also means fiery and hot. In other words, it's the way we pursue and hunger for more of the Spirit that keeps our fire burning. This is what happened to me when I saw Jesus in 2009, and this is what is going to happen to you as you read this book. A relentless pursuit of God will ignite a fire in your heart that will burn unquenched as long as you continue to seek Him.

Back then, in 2009, I hadn't even preached my first sermon yet. To be honest, after being saved for just over a year, I found the Bible to be a complex book, and out-right daunting. I was just a single, twenty-three-year-old young lady on fire for God. I had read about this present Jesus throughout the Bible, and I wanted to experience

Him for myself. So please don't think that if you are not in ministry, you are disqualified from being eligible to experience a face-to-face encounter with Jesus. I loved the assurance that came with knowing that when I leave this earth, I will have my eternal reward in heaven. More important, I also knew that I didn't want to wait until heaven to experience Jesus. I wanted to experience Him right here on earth.

I was tired of the Sunday morning monotony of the usual church schedule.

I was tired of just reading about Jesus encounters.

I wanted to experience a Jesus encounter for myself.

I wanted MORE.

And more was exactly what I got.

Prior to my encounter, I had been praying for months to experience Jesus whereby I could literally see Him. And for all those months, it seemed like He was ignoring me. I prayed constantly, and yet the only thing He would tell me was, "I'm coming."

"But when, Lord?" I would ask. I became so frustrated in my prayers to see Him that at one point I decided that I wouldn't pray for that anymore. However, I soon snapped out of it once I realized that my desire to experience Him in a new way superseded my disappointment in not knowing when He was coming. I decided to keep pursuing Him. When you are truly desperate for God, you will have to make a conscious decision to go after Him even when you don't feel Him.

That entire day, May 16, I prayed, I worshipped, I

repented of all my sins. Everything in me longed for more of the Lord. My desire for Jesus was so intense that I felt like I would burst! But toward the end of the night, I became hungrier for food than I have ever been in my life. My insides felt like they were caving in, and it was only day one of my fast! I had no idea how I would make it through another two days with only water. I even went to my mother and told her that maybe I should eat. She said, "No, you will be okay." I'm forever grateful that she told me that I should continue on my fast. Had I eaten, I'm certain that I would have missed my moment of visitation. And no, it's not about the food; it's about the fact that Jesus wanted to know if I was desperate enough to go after Him when my flesh didn't desire to. I had committed to that time of fasting, and I knew that I had to follow through with it.

That night before I went to bed, I wrote in my notebook about how much I enjoyed unrestrained time with the Lord to seek His face all day. I wrote and told the Lord how much I loved Him and how much I wanted Him more than anything else. I remember feeling such joy and fulfillment in my heart just to be in His presence and be close to Him. Nothing in the world mattered to me more than pleasing the Lord.

Let me just stop for a minute and say, What about you? How badly do you want Him? How badly do you want to encounter Jesus in a new way? Know this: If you want to be closer to the Lord, then you will be, but you must put in the work. The only hindrance stopping you from becoming closer to the Lord is you.

After reading the Bible and journaling, I lay down around midnight to go to sleep. I remember that I felt such an amazing peace as I lay in bed before I dozed off. After spending all day in prayer and worship, I was looking forward to a good night's rest. My mind was still focused on Jesus, and seeing Him and encountering Him in a new way. I didn't know when He was coming to visit me, but I knew that He was.

That night, I was awakened out of my sleep by a blinding light. Think of how bright the light seems after sitting in a completely dark room. Well, imagine that brightness multiplied by 10,000! I had to keep my eyes closed for a moment because of the intensity of the light. After I opened them, I saw a lion's head floating in the air. The lion spoke to me and said, "I am the Lion of Judah." I couldn't believe my eyes! This was not just a vision or a dream. The Lion of Judah was actually in my room looking at me! One key thing that became important to me in the coming months was the fact that the Lion's mouth was closed. The Lord did not have to open his mouth to talk to me.

The room was full of a sound like that of many rushing waters, like ocean waves coming in every direction at the same time. This portion of the encounter became even more significant to me later as I learned through Scripture that the Lord's voice is accompanied by the sound of many waters (Revelation 1:15; 14:12; Ezekiel

43:2). Every particle in the room was visible to my eyes. The air was so tangible that it looked as if I could have literally held every atom in my hand. Next to me, there was an actual scroll floating. This became even more significant to me after I learned that the Book of Revelation states that the Lion of the tribe of Judah is the only one worthy to open the seals of the scroll (Revelation 5:2–5).

Although I was present in my natural body, my spirit was out of my body. I had full awareness of where I was, but it was as if I were literally in two places at the same time—in my natural body as well as in the spiritual realm, similar to what Paul described in 2 Corinthians 12:1–3. I don't know how long the Lord was in my room, but I do know that when He left, my spirit returned to my body, and my room was just as it was before.

I love sharing this encounter because not only did the Lord allow me to experience unimaginable things, but he then showed me the confirmation of my encounter through the Scriptures. I'm so happy Jesus allowed me to experience Him in that capacity early on and was patient with me as He showed me His truth in Scripture.

It wasn't until I had a conversation with my husband about that encounter with Jesus that it brought clarity to some things I had experienced but still didn't understand. When I told him about hearing what sounded like the waves of an ocean in my room, Jonathan mentioned the Scripture concerning the Lord's voice sounding like many waters. If it were not for my husband's ability to hear something relative to the supernatural and associate it with Scripture, I wouldn't have had the scriptural confirmation I needed. I would have, likewise, not been able to understand what the Scripture was saying about the Lord's voice, had I not had the supernatural encounter. I needed both for a full understanding. The supernatural and Scripture are equally important. They are not separate, and they are not at odds.

In the next several pages, my husband will bring scriptural significance to the supernatural so that the supernatural occurrences won't just excite you, but will also ground you in the Word of God.

SEEING THE SCRIPTURE THROUGH THE LENS OF THE SUPERNATURAL

The way you approach Scripture means everything. First off, the Bible is not written in chronological order. Because of this, it's very possible to read Scripture cover to cover and still not understand it. This is why Jesus taught in John 5:39 that we should search the Scriptures, which literally means to thoroughly investigate. Another reason is that according to 2 Corinthians 3:14–16, there is a veil over the hearts of those who read Scripture until they turn to Christ. This is also why when Jesus taught us to investigate the Scriptures in John 5:39, He also gave the reason:

He said that the Scriptures testify about Him. You see, the Bible is a supernatural book. It's supernatural because it's a person. Jesus is the Word, and when we read the Word, it should lead us to Him (John 1:1).

Many approach the Bible to learn about God. However, the problem is that the only way to learn something new is to associate it with something you already know. This is one of the reasons Jesus taught with parables. This is also why encountering God for yourself is important. Only then does it change the way you approach what you learn of Him in the Scriptures. You see, there's a difference between reading the Word and reading the Word with a prophetic eye: reading Scripture through the lens of the supernatural. Romans 10:17 teaches that faith comes by hearing and hearing comes by the Word of God. What many do not realize is that this Scripture deals with a lot more than merely hearing through the Word of God. It actually has a lot to do with our ability to see in the Spirit. It's how God created faith to function in our lives.

Let me show you how. Scientists have proven that the part of our brain that supports our ability to hear is the same part of our brain from which our imagination functions. It's called the pineal gland. This is key because our imagination has a lot to do with our spiritual sight. In fact, Ephesians 1:16 teaches that God wants to enlighten the eyes of our understanding. In the Greek language, the word *understanding* is actually defined as imagination. This means that our imagination represents our ability to see in the Spirit rather than our imagination representing something that is not real.

Now don't get me wrong; our spiritual sight is not limited to our imagination. But it does begin there for many. There are actually seven different definitions for the word *vision* in the Hebraic language. They all represent different degrees of spiritual sight that I'll explain later. I'll also show you nine ways to increase your spiritual sight. But for now I want you to understand that you have probably been taught wrong about your imagination. For so long we have been told that our imagination is something that is fictional. However, our imagination is actually what gives us the potential to experience what can take place in the spiritual dimension. Some of us may have even been taught that our imagination is evil. But Scripture doesn't teach that. Scripture teaches us only that we are to cast down the specific imaginations that are, in fact, vain. This means that every imagination is not vain, neither should all imagination be discredited. In fact, the Scripture doesn't merely teach us to cast down the imaginations that are vain but also tells us which specific imaginations we should consider vain: these are the ones that exalt themselves above the knowledge of God's Word. It's key for us to understand this, because our faith will be hindered to the degree that our imagination is.

I've discovered that one of the most powerful things I can do when reading the Word of God is to imagine what I'm reading while reading. I've also concluded that faith is not faith until it is free to imagine what it is believing God for. You see, faith in and of itself is supernatural in nature. We do ourselves a great disservice when we remove the supernatural out of the context of God's word. The only Scripture in the Bible that defines directly what faith is describes it as the substance and evidence of the invisible world (Hebrews 11:1–3). I want to show you some things in Scripture that we overlook as they relate to the supernatural. As I do, I want you to use your imagination and try to think of how witnessing these things in biblical accounts would have been and how it would have impacted you. I believe that as you do, your faith will be strengthened and you will have more ability to believe the supernatural in your life. I believe it's going to create an appetite for more of what you are going to begin experiencing. And aren't we supposed to long for more?

Now here are the rules. I don't want you to skip over a story title that you may be familiar with. Read each story and see how it is laced with supernatural reality. We are going to look at some of the popular biblical themes. As we do, I'm going to give a short synopsis of some of the supernatural activity I see taking place that many may overlook. Lastly, we will look at the life of Jesus.

MORE THAN FIRE FROM HEAVEN: ELIJAH

Everyone loves the story of Elijah calling fire down from heaven. It was quite a phenomenon even then. The only glitch in the story is how often we communicate it as being a once-in-a-lifetime encounter for Elijah. I was a little disappointed when I realized that Elijah was pretty much known for calling down fire from heaven on multiple occasions. In fact, Scriptures record him doing so at least four times. Not only was the man known for summoning fire from heaven, but he was also known for disappearing and teleporting to different locations. He was even awakened by an angel, who then cooked him dinner. The food was so supernatural that Scripture says his body was nourished by that one meal for a total of forty days! Can you imagine eating a dinner that gradually keeps filling you and nourishing you for forty days?

Even more, through prayer, Elijah could control weather patterns. And I don't even want to elaborate on how he could run at the speed of a Porsche (1 Kings 18:46).

MORE THAN SEVEN PLAGUES AND THE PARTING OF THE RED SEA: MOSES

As they pertain to Moses, most of the Ten Commandments movies focus only on the seven plagues of Egypt and the parting of the Red Sea. Those were incredible events in their own right, but there was a lot more going on in the supernatural with Moses.

Bringing the Israelites out of Egypt, God was with Moses in such a supernatural way that the Scripture says there was a cloud that guided them by day and a fire that guided them by night. What made it even more supernatural was the fact that the cloud and the fire were so huge in the sky that both the Israelites and the Egyptians were able to see them. Can you imagine seeing a cloud suspended over a nation, which then shape-shifts into a fire by nightfall right in front of your eyes? This thing was so significant that the Scriptures talk of how every nation of the earth heard of it and feared God.

But it goes deeper than that. This was no natural phenomenon in the sky. God Himself was in the cloud and in the fire. By the time Israel was in the wilderness, God would visit them, appearing on a mountain in both the cloud and the fire at the same time. Not only that, but God Himself would speak through the cloud and be heard *audibly* by every single person in the wilderness.

MORE THAN A TOWER TO HEAVEN: NIMROD AND THE TOWER OF BABEL

Many know the story of the Tower of Babel. It was when God confused the language of men to keep them from building a tower to heaven. The end of the story . . . right? I think not. The reality is that those people were trying to build a tower to heaven, and God Himself said that they would have accomplished it had He not stopped them. Do you know what this means?

It means that their technological advances were far beyond our modern technology. It means that they were accomplishing something that NASA is still trying to figure out. NASA, Elon Musk, Steve Jobs, and Apple Inc. have nothing on these people. But what's more supernatural is how they possibly could have gotten this information. The only insight we have into this possibility is the life of Enoch. Before I go there, you must understand that there are many false Scriptures that did not make the Bible for a reason. There are other books that the Bible itself mentions, which can be trusted although they are not included in Scripture. One of those books is the Book of Enoch, which is even quoted from in the New Testament. It talks about how men, during the time when the fallen angels were intermingling with men and creating a hybrid species, were taught various things, including super-advanced technology. Yes, the Bible talks about that! Incredible, right?

MORE THAN GIANTS IN THE EARTH: ANGELS AND THE SONS OF MEN

It's clear that there were giants in the earth. Everyone accepts that reality, especially in the context of David confronting Goliath. However, the origin of those giants is what we kind of smooth over in our teaching. We rarely emphasize the fact that the giants in the earth were a hybrid species. They were a species created through human intercourse with fallen angels, those who had rebelled against God.

Now before you get disturbed at that reality, you have to understand why I personally love to emphasize this. It brings relevance to how authentic a supernatural encounter is. It doesn't get any more tangible than making babies. You see, the supernatural merging into our world is so tangible in nature that it is not something that we merely experience in our dimension only. There is a dimension of the supernatural that merges so fully into our world that we do have direct interaction in ways that are tangible in nature. And let me assure you, that dimension of the supernatural is not just real; it is actually more real than the natural dimension we live in.

Don't worry. I will explain the reality of this supernatural dimension in more detail later. For now, let's look at the life of Jesus, because He is where we find our anchor in these things. Above all else, the supernatural is ultimately about knowing Jesus more.

Jesus is the supernatural, and as we consider His lifestyle, we see traces of otherworldly activity that's quite frankly pretty mind blowing. I mean, no wonder He had everyone's attention. He was doing a lot more than healing the sick and raising the dead and multiplying food.

MORE THAN WORKING MIRACLES AND FEEDING MULTITUDES: JESUS

Jesus was a living, breathing, walking example of what it meant to live in this world and yet live in another world at the same time. He lived in two realms. He accessed another dimension. Let's look at just some of the examples. His very birth was announced by angels, and it literally changed the constellations. We think the solar eclipse and blood moons were something, but the signs in the heavens were so vividly pointing to the arrival of a new world leader at the birth of Jesus that a heathen king put out an order to kill babies. In that day, it was genocide. In our day, it's abortion. The signs in the sky literally had King Herod nervous that another king was being born to overthrow his government. He believed it. Think about that. This was not a YouTube video about the illuminati or some random conspiracy theory, but rather a sequence of supernatural events about ancient biblical prophecies of the birth of Jesus that even garnered the attention of a heathen king.

And just in case you don't believe that it was supernatural enough for the stars of heaven to align around his birth through a virgin woman, let's look at some of their details. Both the entrance and the exit of Jesus in this world were on a grand scale. The ministry of Jesus was so supernatural that it didn't begin with a first sermon or ordination service. Jesus' ministry literally began with an open announcement from heaven at His baptism service in the Jordan River with a booming voice that declared: "This is My beloved Son, in whom I am well pleased" (Matthew 3:17). And it didn't stop there. Jesus more than once had His ministry confirmed by an open and audible voice from heaven that was witnessed by others as well. You must understand that Jesus was not just claiming some type of supernatural encounter with God in a vision or claiming to be sent by God the Father with a message. No. This was actually God the Father Himself openly confirming who Jesus was and letting others witness it.

Let's take a look at two examples. In Luke 9, Jesus goes up on a mountain and heaven announces who He is again after his original baptism encounter. Peter, James, and John are there to witness this particular account. However, what sends them over the top is that this time they are not just witnessing God the Father speaking openly from heaven. This time they literally witness Jesus' body and clothing begin to glow in plain sight. Can you imagine it? Can you imagine seeing so much of the glory of God on an individual that His physical appearance changed and began to glow like the sun right there in front of your eyes? And just in case that doesn't suffice, it happens a third time in John 12, where an entire multitude hears the voice that is talking.

Do you understand how mind blowing that is for innocent bystanders? Just imagine that you ask God a question in public and He answers so loudly that everyone around you hears the answer. You would never pray again in your life, "God, help me hear Your voice more clearly." You would *know* how to hear. Or what about when Jesus tells Nathaniel that he would see the heavens open and the constant activity of angels going in and out of heaven in John 1:50–51?

There are so many other examples. One of my favorites is found in Mark 6:46–52. It's the story of Jesus walking on the water in the midst of a storm while His disciples were in the boat having a panic attack. Surely, walking on water was enough on its own. But the more I look at this text, the more supernatural activity I see that we fail to recognize. And to top it off, not only were the literal facts surrounding the story extremely supernatural in nature, but I believe the story itself is prophetically symbolic of where the church is today. Let's look at the story and I'll show you what I mean.

And when he had sent them away, he departed into a mountain to pray. And when even was come, the ship was in the midst of the sea, and he alone on the land. And he saw them toiling in rowing; for the wind was contrary unto them: and about the fourth watch of the night he cometh unto them, walking upon the sea, and would have passed by them. But when they saw him walking upon the sea, they supposed it had been a spirit, and cried out: For they all saw him, and were troubled. And immediately he talked with them, and saith unto them, Be of good cheer: it is I; be not afraid. And he went up unto them into the ship; and the wind ceased:

and they were sore amazed in themselves beyond measure, and wondered. (Mark 6:46–51)

Now, I understand how very easy it is to read the previous text as if it were a Sunday school lesson and completely miss the significance of the supernatural in it. So, let me dissect it piece by piece. First of all, notice that Jesus sent His disciples ahead of Him in a boat at sea while He remained in prayer. We don't know how long the prayer was exactly except for the fact that evening had come while He was praying. And not only did evening come while He was praying, but according to the Book of Matthew's account of this same story, Jesus didn't finish praying until the fourth watch of the night, which is anywhere between 3 a.m. and 6 a.m. This means that Jesus had begun praying during the day and didn't finish until many hours later, early the next morning. Why is this important? Because how in the world did Jesus end up finding the boat hours after they had already been at sea; and on top of that, He did so while walking. This would be equivalent to outrunning the *Titanic* at sea. Or outswimming it. Impossible. Something supernatural happened here.

First off, the highest mileage a rowboat has ever been recorded at is 13 mph. This is light-years faster than any swimmer. Not only that, but the disciples had a head start of many hours; and yet Jesus still managed to leave His prayer time and immediately catch up to them. And to top it off, Jesus was *walking*. There had to be some type of supernatural transportation going on there. One second Jesus was on the mountain, and the next moment He was mid-sea in the middle of the storm walking on water. Jesus was literally walking through a storm that would toss an ocean liner like the *Titanic* around like a paper plate. He walked through winds that twelve men couldn't row a boat through. He could have teleported inside the boat, but He chose to transport Himself just close enough to the boat so that He would have to walk on water the rest of the way through the storm.

It gets deeper. The text clearly says in the account in Matthew that the boat was in the midst of the sea. However, from the mountain, Jesus was able to see exactly where the boat was and navigate to their location, as if He had the sight of an eagle to see multiple miles off (Mark 6:46–48). Not only that, but the average person can hardly see through the windshield of their car in a bad storm with windshield wipers on. Jesus was multiple miles away, looking through the storm, and prophetically located exactly where the disciples' boat was. This was supernatural enough, but then Scripture says that when the disciples saw Jesus, they thought He was a ghost or a spirit. The only explanation I have is that His physical appearance had changed here in the same way it changed on the Mount of Transfiguration, in Luke 9. It makes sense especially since they both happened in the context of Jesus praying *beforehand*.

It is quite possible that the physical appearance of Jesus was translucent. While you mull that over, the more important focus of the text is how symbolic this particular "seeing Jesus as a ghost" portion is to where the church is now. Jesus is passing by our boats in a supernatural way in the middle of a storm, but we are treating Him like a ghost. What I mean by this is that we have trained our minds to be more superstitious than open to the supernatural. People will see a psychic before they will acknowledge the prophetic. They would rather interpret zodiac signs than embrace the anointing of the sons of Issachar, and properly understand and interpret the times and seasons (1 Chronicles 12:32).

And again the supernatural came into play at Jesus' death. According to the Scriptures, the graves of the saints were opened right after He died; they rose from the dead (!) and appeared to many. Can you imagine that? Patriarchs and matriarchs who you've heard of coming to you and saying, "Hello, I'm Esther." "Hello, I'm King David." The Bible declares it! Think of how eternity invaded the earth at the very moment when Jesus sacrificed His body as an offering. Literally the entire world came under the same time zone and there was darkness over the entire earth for the space of an hour. It so shifted time that we must now recognize time by BC and AD.

I reference the life and death of Jesus when examining the supernatural for a reason. Jesus Himself said that He has sent us into the world in the exact same way He was sent into the world. First John also says, "...as he is, so are we in this world" (4:17). I believe there's a different dimension in the supernatural now opening to the Body of Christ. It's so much more than just miracles and signs and wonders. It's a lifestyle of living in the supernatural and cultivating a relationship with God that far exceeds any love or ecstasy we could ever imagine. This is going to be so important as we move ahead, because most of us read about the life of Jesus and embrace the supernatural only in the context of miracles. However, the reality is that there was so much more taking place. And I believe that is what God wants to show us today.

This may be completely new to you or you may be a believer who has embraced the supernatural already. Whatever the case may be, God is calling you to go deeper with Him. Will you say yes to His call?

CHAPTER 3

WORLDS BEYOND OUR WORLD

When God invites us to know Him, He also invites us into His world. This is why seeking a relationship with Him includes seeking His Kingdom. God instructs us to seek His Kingdom because there are things we will not understand about Him if we do not understand the world He lives in.

There is another world, and it's supernatural. The more we understand how that world operates, the more clearly we will grasp the way God moves. We will also understand how and why He does some of the things He does. There are worlds beyond what our natural eyes can see and even beyond the galaxies known to scientific research. More specifically, it is a world of worlds. That's the best way to describe heaven. A world of worlds. I know because I've been there. I'll explain that later, but for now just know that it's a literal dimension beyond the natural world that literally consists of places that are inhabited.

Let me first begin with why I call heaven a "world of worlds." The earth is only an extension of God's world. You must understand that what distinguishes the earth from heaven is not that the earth is material and tangible but heaven is rather not. The heavens are more physical than the earth, and not because the earth is any less physical than what we think it is. Rather, it's that heaven has a more superior form of matter. Heaven is an actual physical place. Yes, it is a spiritual reality, but not a spiritual reality like what we assume spiritual realities are. But before I go any further, let's start at the beginning and work our way back to this point.

A WORLD OF WORLDS

The first time "heaven" is mentioned in the Bible, the word is in plural form. This is why the majority of the time the New Testament mentions heaven, it mentions its plurality as "heavenly places of heavenly realms." Is there more than one heaven? No, not in the sense of good people may go to one heaven and bad people go to another. Of course not. When we consider heaven, we must consider it in the vastness of its most expanded condition. For example, the Scriptures teach about heavens above the heavens, and the heavens of the heavens. In other words, heaven has heavens. Again, this is what I mean by a "world of worlds." The best way to look at it is to consider how one continent in the earth can host many nations. That nation can in turn host many states or provinces. Those states can then host many cities, and its cities many communities. Start applying the word *vast* when you think of the heavens.

But what about how many galaxies there are? And what about how many solar systems can be represented in just one galaxy? Have you ever thought about how scientists call the vastness of space "galaxies," but the Scriptures call them "heavens"? The reality is that heaven is yet beyond that. Let me explain.

Before I get into my out-of-body encounters, there are some details that I won't get into for three reasons. One, I've read too many books on the supernatural where the author does not point to literal biblical references in his or her explanation of their various encounters. Therefore, my goal is to balance my personal experiences in the supernatural with scriptural teaching concerning what the supernatural is all about. Two, if I go into too much detail of my encounter, it will keep me from being able to expound more fully biblically on a portion of the encounter I'd like to use to bring more scriptural clarity to supernatural encounters across the board. In other words, I will explain some encounters in detail and I will cherry-pick certain aspects of other encounters for a greater purpose. If you find yourself wanting more, you can always take our online course on the subject by visiting unquenchedthebook.com. Three, I won't go into detail about some encounters because every chapter is going to feature a supernatural encounter. Before you're finished reading this book, you'll read about many encounters in detail because they are relevant to the scriptural truth my wife and I desire to highlight in this book. The emphasis is not on every detail of every encounter, but rather how supernatural encounters can deepen your hunger for and understanding of the Word of God.

A COUPLE OF KEYS FROM MY TRIPS TO HEAVEN

Over the years, I've had a couple of experiences where I was very aware that I was out of my body. In one of my out-of-body experiences, while at home, I actually saw my natural body lying on the floor before I got back inside of it. I was not dead, near death, or sick. I simply had a supernatural encounter with God. During a couple of these occurrences in which God took me out of my body, I went to heaven. The more shocking reality is that I did not just end up in heaven. I actually experienced myself traveling out of this natural world into the spirit world. Yep, I was literally flying upward, outside of my body, until I reached the place we call heaven. More specifically, I was being carried away by the Spirit of God into the heavenly dimension. Just in case that sounds bizarre, what I'm sharing of being carried away in the Spirit happened to people throughout the Bible. It happened to Ezekiel in almost every other chapter of his book in the Bible. It also happened to Philip in the New Testament. The reality is that every time someone was carried away in the Spirit, it was not to heaven. At times it was actually to different parts of the earth.

We live in a three-dimensional world, but even scientists know that there are dimensions beyond the three we recognize our natural world by. No matter what scientific terms they give, whether black matter, quantum physics, etc., the truth is that any reality or force outside of our three-dimensional reality exists within the heavenly dimension. The phenomenon is that these spiritual dimensions *can* be detected from our natural dimension. But scientists can't fully crack the code on the existence of other dimensions because these dimensions must be perceived by the same source from which they exist: the Spirit of God.

I know there is a superior reality. I know, because I've experienced it firsthand. I can save myself years of studying quantum physics because of this. No scientist on the planet can tell me how I flew out of my bed, through my roof, above the sky, bypassing galaxies, to reach the heavens. Why? Because it's supernatural. Only the Scriptures can explain what science can't. And only the supernatural can give us an understanding of things in the Scriptures that either seem to contradict or leave us completely clueless in our comprehension of God and His Word.

CAUGHT UP

It was through these occurrences in which I was taken to heaven that I began to understand what Paul meant in 2 Corinthians 12:3–6 where he mentioned being "caught up." I've discovered that the "caught up" experience is an experience in and of itself, and not just the reality of being in heaven. It is literally the feeling of traveling up into the heavenly dimension.

Another thing that I took home from my very first experience of being caught up into heaven is that I by-passed galaxies to get to an actual place, a literal place. Try to think of heaven as a planet, not because it's merely a planet, but because there are some heavenly realities that there are no earthly terms for. So, we have to use comparisons to understand them. In this case, considering heaven in the context of planets is the only thing I can think of that will help you grasp how physical and literal heavenly places are. However, heaven is not just a place; it's also a dimension. That is what makes it so supernatural. After all, it is a supernatural world.

HEAVEN IS MORE THAN WE THINK

The point is that heaven is far beyond what we have been taught. The Bible has a lot to say about God's world, and honestly, we do a great disservice in our attempts to explain heaven and we often misrepresent the Scriptures terribly while doing so. Our vague attempts to explain heaven can even be quite boring. Imagine someone, who has never been there, trying to explain the ancient Coliseum of Rome or an African safari or even a city zoo. They will fail on all accounts to give a full and accurate picture. Yes, you can read about accounts from those who wrote about heaven in the Scriptures, but there are certain details you will always miss since you're taking it in secondhand.

I've been there. And though it was brief, the little I did see, and the little I experienced in the process of being allowed to see, gave me a lot more clarity about the reality of heaven than what many have made it out to be. Heaven is not just one place or just one big space. It is not a place where we bow down and worship God all day. We are not meant to be one dimensional in our relationship with Him. The very beauty, luxuries, delicacies, adventure, art, culture, and landscapes that make up heaven all worship God in and of themselves.

We are not going to be in heaven telling God that He is holy for all eternity. Are you serious? God is not that boring. I love to worship God and am not implying that our expressions of worship are boring, but I do want you to think and reconsider some things about what we will actually be experiencing in heaven.

HEAVEN'S CIVILIZATION

When the Scriptures say that God created the heavens, the word *created* literally means to sculpt and design. Scripture also refers to God as an architect and master builder (Hebrews 11:10). Heaven is full of things that serve as the prototype of things we experience on earth. In fact, everything on earth that is of any worth or value was derived from heaven (James 1:17; Ecclesiastes 1:9). All the concepts of livelihood, culture, and civilization originated in the heavens. In fact, the culture of heaven is far more advanced than that of the earth.

The following chart consists of a list of things in the earth that originated in heaven.

Mountains	(Revelation 21:10)
Rivers	(Revelation 22:1)
Trees	(Revelation 22:2)
Mansions	(John 14:2)
Animals	(Revelation 6:2, 4, 8)
Streets	(Revelation 21:21)
Gates and Walls	(Revelation 21:10-11)
Food	(Luke 22:30; Psalm 78:23)
Cities and Geographical Locations	(Hebrews 11:10; Hebrews 12:22)

The Scriptures also teach that God did not just create the heavens, but He literally stretched the heavens. Heaven is a lot more creative and interesting than what it is normally projected to be. If we could imagine the earth in all its beauty and in its original state before sin entered in, we would only begin to grasp the splendor and wonder of heaven.

The heavenly city mentioned in the previous scriptural references is a great example of how vast heaven is. The city is only one of eight literal places or geographical locations in heaven mentioned in Scripture. In fact, the Scriptures also speak of a heavenly country or nation (Hebrews 11:14–16). To be a country, it would have to consist of multiple cities, states, and regions.

The following chart consists of seven additional references of geographical locations in heaven that will help us embrace heaven's creative makeup:

Seven Other Places in Heaven:	
Paradise/Resorts	(2 Corinthians 12:2-4; Revelation 2:7)
The Throne Room/ Council Room	(Revelation 4–5)
The Holy Mountain	(Psalms 15:1; 87)
The True Heavenly Sanctuary	Hebrews 8:2, 5-6; Acts 7:44)

Seven Other Places in Heaven:	
The Storehouses/Warehouses	(Deuteronomy 28:12; Psalm 33:6-7)
The Father's House/ Many Mansions	(John 14:2)
The Banquet Houses, Rooms, and Tables	(Songs of Solomon 2:4; Luke 22:30)

THE STRUCTURE OF GOD'S WORLD

In the beginning, God created the heavens and the earth. That's what the Bible begins with because that's what happened. This means that the creation of the heavens preceded the creation of the earth. Consider this. The creation of the earth was so elaborate and detailed that it was explained over the course of a seven-day period. Do you really think the creation of the heavens was any less elaborate than that? I think not.

Heaven is not a world of clouds, angels, and bright white lights. Its architecture is beyond our current knowledge and understanding. Its culture is vibrant and dynamic, and its civilization is advanced beyond anything we've ever known. How do we know this? It goes back to the Word of God. There are only a few men who looked into eternity before time began and saw the beginning. Moses was one; Paul was another. And they both wrote about their experiences.

The difference between Moses and Paul is that when Moses wrote, he focused more on the creation of the earth. Paul focused more on the creation of the heavens. In Colossians, Paul describes the layout and structure of how the heavens were created. However, he primarily saw a governmental structure and hierarchy of angels that make up the protocol of how heaven is governed. Let's examine Colossians 1:16 in more detail:

For by him were all things created, that are in heaven, and that are in earth, visible and invisible, whether they be thrones, or dominions, or principalities, or powers: all things were created by him, and for him.

Here, Paul's reference deals with a succession of authorities and rank in the realm of the Spirit. This succession of authority is descriptive of the governmental structure among the angelic Kingdoms. This passage alone literally gives us insight into how sophisticatedly structured the heavens were. God literally created a world, called it heaven, and structured it like a kingdom. This Scripture is showing us a governing body in the Spirit world consisting of angelic beings and angelic structures, especially since they were the primary inhabitants of heaven in the beginning. And so, moving forward, the order of angels is one thing we need to reference to understand the culture of heaven.

What Paul saw in Colossians was dealing not only with a governing structure but also with the spiritual protocol that governed territories and delegated authorities in the Spirit world. Let's briefly decipher what each represents. Thrones represent positions of mastery and sovereign rulership from which law and judgment are administered. The thrones in Scripture are comparable to the Supreme Court's representation in America. Dominions represent territories and various jurisdictions. Lastly, principalities represent jurisdictional headship and do not exist without princes and delegated governing powers or deputies.

Just as we have presidents, kings, and governors in the natural world, there are angels that operate as royal delegates with territories and jurisdictions from which they govern. In fact, Jude 6 informs us that in the heavens there are estates and habitation that were created for the angels to dwell in. The word *estate* in Jude 6 is defined as "land," "territory," and "abode." The word *habitation* is defined as "abode" and "housing." This means that the heavens in which the angels live are literally civilized.

Scripture also teaches that there are so many angels that they cannot be numbered or counted (Hebrews 12:22). This means that there would have to be multiple territories, communities, and divisions of this "innumerable" company of angels. Although we do not know the extent of this fact, we do know that the heavens in which the angels reside are very structured.

Heaven is no fable or fairytale existence. It is clearly a highly advanced, highly civilized, and highly sophisticatedly designed world.

HEAVEN IS THE REAL WORLD

All of this is just a little insight into what God created in the beginning, but it goes deeper. The reality is that heaven is the superior world. Let that truth sink in. And if all of this is true and literal, there are some facts about the invisible dimension that we need to rethink. As we do, it will help us embrace the reality of what we've learned about heaven so far and embrace its reality like never before.

This brings me back to one of my opening statements: "The earth is only an extension of God's world." I want you to consider God's world of worlds in a way that will help you understand the extent of what you are getting yourself into when you begin pursuing God and asking Him to show you things about His supernatural world.

Are you ready to crack the code to the mysteries of heaven? They are, in fact, the mysteries of the supernatural world.

SPIRITUAL REALITIES OF HEAVEN

Some of my favorite Scriptures concerning spiritual realities are found in the Book of Hebrews. Hebrews 8:5

tells us: "Who serve unto the example and *shadow of heavenly things*, as Moses was admonished of God when he was about to make the tabernacle: for, See, saith he, that thou *make all things according to the pattern shewed to thee in the mount*" (emphasis added). It's interesting to note that the phrase *of heavenly things* in the original language literally means "of true existence." This means that the things of heaven are those that are of true existence and reality. If we are going to truly embrace a scriptural understanding of heaven, we must begin by understanding that heaven's state of existence is far more superior to that of earth.

The Scripture says this verbatim in Hebrews 10:34, which is my favorite Scripture concerning the reality of heaven. According to the Scripture, in heaven we have a better and more enduring substance. When the Scriptures mention the better substance in heaven, the word *substance* literally means property, goods, and possessions.

That's a lot to take in, so let me make it plain before I move on. The Scripture is literally saying that the substance that makes up heaven is better than the substance that makes up earth. This is why Hebrews 11:3 teaches that the things we see were made by things we do not see. It's because what we do not see is more substantial. This brings me to my next point.

THREE THINGS WE MUST CHANGE IN OUR VIEW OF SPIRITUAL THINGS

The first thing we need to understand is that spiritual does not mean nonphysical. Spiritual things are not merely figments of our imagination. They are more real than our reality. The things we do not see are used to create the things we do see. The natural world is not the only physical world. Remember, in heaven we have a better substance, according to Hebrews 10:34. It is when we learn the secrets of the supernatural that we can began to see spiritual things literally materialize and take on form in the world we live in.

In the Book of Genesis, the spiritual world was so physical that fallen angels impregnated women, who gave birth to a hybrid species called giants. It was so real in the life of Abraham that angels feasted on a dinner he had prepared for them. For Elijah, it was the opposite. An angel actually delivered a meal to him that he ate, which then strengthened him to go on a forty-day journey without needing to eat again in between. The spiritual realm was so physical that King Herod died in Acts 12 because of how an angel touched him. The list goes on. The point is that we must stop separating what's physical and what's not by what's natural and what's spiritual. We can no longer equate spiritual to intangible.

Another truth of spiritual realities is that something invisible is not something that cannot be seen. "Invisible" does not mean that you "cannot see it," but rather you "do not see it" *yet*. The Scripture teaches us in 2 Corinthians 4:16–17 that we can look at things that are not seen. This is what happened in 2 Kings 6 when God opened the eyes of Elisha's servant.

The third view we need to challenge is that all imagination is fake. In fact, because of what I understand about the power of our imagination, I like the phrase *make believe* in reference to our imagination. If we have faith and work out our imagination long enough, it will "make what we believe." There is power in our imagination, and there is an important reason we have it. It is a creative engine in the spirit world, and when we utilize it, Ephesians 3:20 teaches that God likes to take it and exceed it. The imagination is but the potential of the supernatural. If we can think it, God can do more than what we think. If it can exist in our minds, it can be done by God's hands. God often uses the imagination as the bridge between the natural and the spiritual worlds.

If it exists in our mind as imagination, it exists in the spiritual world as a thing. This is why 2 Corinthians 10 correlates the imagination to "high things." 2 Corinthians 10 does not just mention the reality of vain imaginations; it also defines explicitly which imaginations are, in fact, vain. Those imaginations are scripturally defined as thoughts, ideas, philosophies, fantasies, or any other knowledge that attempts to exalt itself over the knowledge of God. All other imaginations that do not breach those boundaries? God intends to use them. The primary way that God uses our imagination is in our faith and in our spiritual sight. Our imagination plays a huge role in how we embrace spiritual realities.

This in no way means that the experience of the supernatural is some abstract experience. Neither is it limited to something that you merely experience in your mind. As you begin to understand your imagination more, you will learn that what begins in your mind is designed to materialize in the world. This is not mind over matter; it is matter over mind. It is more real than real can ever be.

The supernatural is at work around us all the time, and the experience of it includes nothing short of the involvement of all of our God-given sensory capabilities. To know God in a supernatural way is not something that we experience in our mind or in our beliefs but something we experience with everything that we are and every fiber of our being.

WHERE GOD'S WORLD AND OUR WORLD MEET

God created a world, structured it as a Kingdom, and called it heaven. He then made the earth as an extension of His world and decided that man would rule here as part of His eternal family. He created the earth to reflect how he made the heavens. He wanted the earth to reflect His Kingdom in the heavens. He wanted there to be a constant interaction between heaven and earth. A marrying of the two.

According to Matthew 6:10, God wants things on the earth just like they are in the heavens. However, this is the dimension we were locked out of when Adam sinned. This is why we must be born of the Spirit in order to see and enter the Kingdom of God, which is the heavenly dimension on earth (John 3). This is why I mentioned earlier that heaven is not just a place that is beyond the stars. It is also a dimension. It's a mystery understood only by the Spirit of God. According to Scripture, the Kingdom of heaven is not just a place beyond the stars. Yes, it is a literal place, but remember, it is vast and it is supernatural. Jesus always preached and told His disciples to announce that the Kingdom of heaven was at hand, which means it's always around us. He also told them that the Kingdom was within them. This is why Romans 15 teaches that it is an atmosphere in the Holy Spirit. This means it is a literal place in the Holy Spirit.

If you pay attention, the word *heaven* is mentioned in three different contexts in Genesis 1, the creation story. The first is in reference to the immediate abode of God. However, the other two will help you understand the mystery I'm communicating. The second time heaven is mentioned, in Genesis 1:7, it's in reference to the galaxies. The last time it's mentioned, in Genesis 1:21, it's in reference to the air and atmosphere within the earth. It's called the open firmament.

This is where you can reference the term *open heaven* in the Scriptures within the creation account. It is important to do so, because it establishes the reality that open heavens were the original intention of God within the earth. It has to do with where things from the spiritual dimension gain access into the natural world. This happens in the atmosphere. In order for things to move from God's world into our world, they have to come into the earth through the atmosphere. This is what Genesis 1:21 describes our open firmament to be. According to John 3, when supernatural things take place, they happen in the wind, invisible to the naked eye, only seen by the person who is willing to be born again in the Spirit.

When I was taken out of my body, I was taken to the immediate abode of God. Maybe that's why I saw myself shoot beyond the galaxies to get there. However, God wants His abode among men. He wants to experience His Kingdom on the earth now. He doesn't want us to wait until we die to go to heaven. His Kingdom is always around us, though invisible. But remember, invisible does not mean we're not allowed to see something; it just means we're not able to see it. However, there's a reason we don't see into God's supernatural world, realizing His world is alive and active all around us all the time: We are all born spiritually dead due to Adam's sin. We have to be willing to allow God to cause us to be reborn by His Spirit in order to accept the invitation to be welcomed into His world and enjoy an eternal relationship with Him.

It is only as we are born of water and Spirit that we can not only see, but also enter into the Kingdom of God. John 1 teaches that God gave power to as many as received His son Jesus to become the sons of God. As we receive Jesus and allow His Spirit to literally baptize and submerse us into a process of being reborn in the Spirit, we will begin to see and enter the Kingdom of God. We will begin to experience heaven on earth. We've been given an invitation to enter God's world and be with Him and get to know Him as our Father in heaven.

If you have not done so already, pray this simple prayer with me:

Jesus, I believe You are the Son of God. You died for my sins and God raised You from the dead. You are no longer dead. You are alive. By faith I really believe that. I can sense You are real. I receive what You did for me. I receive You into my life. I can't deal with my own sins, but You already did. Now I need Your power to change me and transform my life. Fill me with Your Spirit. Completely submerge my life with Your Spirit and I will never be the same. Send someone into my life to help reinforce this change I'm experiencing right now. Send me someone You trust to help guide me through the next steps I need to take in my journey of getting to know You better. In Your name, Jesus, Amen.

CHAPTER 4

ENTERING GOD'S WORLD

Just like every nation, every world of thought has its own language. Entrepreneurship has a language. The accounting world has a language. The medical field has a language. The supernatural world is no different.

SUPERNATURAL ATMOSPHERE, OPEN HEAVENS, AND CARRYING THE KINGDOM WITHIN

Your success and progress in a specific sphere greatly depend on learning the language of that world. If you tried talking to my accounting firm, you'd learn that very quickly. They get paid to know all the tax terms I have no clue about. Why? Because they are the experts in that field.

In the same way, my wife and I are experts in the supernatural. It's what we're known for. We have experience explaining the supernatural to every type of person, from our children, to the culturally elite, from our house—all the way to the White House. People are drawn to us because we are able to show how the supernatural looks in the daily context of a couple who have a balanced life of marriage, family, and other goals. This is the strength of an expert. We make it look easy.

When you see or read about the supernatural and it becomes weird in a way that causes suspicion, it's because there is either a problem with the communication you're getting or you're simply not dealing with an expert. The purpose of this chapter is to make way for clear communication. We want to remove any barriers and offer foundational truths about entering into and interacting with God's supernatural world so that the supernatural is no longer something foreign to you. We believe that anyone who desires it can know, understand, and experience the supernatural presence and power of God.

OPEN HEAVENS: ATMOSPHERES, SPIRITUAL REALMS, AND THE KINGDOM OF GOD

In earth as it is in heaven. This is what God wants for our lives. This is the Kingdom of God. It is the reality of another world existing simultaneously with our world, waiting on us to interact with it. If it were not so, Jesus would have never told us to make this reality the priority of our prayers in Matthew 6:10. Understanding this is where the knowledge of so many spiritual realities begin to unfold. Let's begin the journey. First off, from now on, when you hear the phrase *Kingdom of God*, you need to think not just heaven, but heaven on earth. What does this mean? Do the streets turn into gold? Does all pain and sorrow leave? No, but it's just as good.

When we speak of heaven on earth, we are speaking of a spiritual dimension—realities that exist beyond the naked eye. In other words, the existence of heaven on the earth is predominately atmospheric. I'll explain this shortly, but for now understand that this is the reality of the Kingdom of God. This Kingdom, or this heaven, is an invisible dimension, and although invisible, it can yet be seen. It's a supernatural world. The origin of this reality is a literal place beyond the galaxies. However, by the Spirit of God, it is a place that directly influences and coexists with the natural world we live in. This is what we call an open heaven. Therefore, let's first examine what an open heaven is and then we can use that foundation to understand atmosphere.

THE OPEN FIRMAMENT OF HEAVEN

In order to understand an open heaven, you have to understand the firmament. It was created in Genesis 1:6

to separate the matter above the earth from the matter within the earth. Scripture also says that God named the firmament "heaven." Afterward, the second firmament created was called the open firmament. The Scriptures often mention open heavens. However, it's not until we reference the Scriptures that mention open heavens, its genesis, and definition of what the firmament is, that we gain insight into what open heavens are.

The facts are that the open firmament, or the open heavens, exists within the sky above us and the air around us, according to Genesis 1:20. This is within the earth's atmosphere. In addition to this, the word *firmament* means "heavens" in its most expanded condition. Remember, there were two firmaments created in creation's account. One was created in what we call outer space, and one literally in the skies above our head.

Therefore, according to the definition of firmament and the historical account of its creation, we discover that the firmament is not merely a separation of the heavens. It is also an extension by which the heavens expand throughout various natural and spiritual territories. Here is where it gets good. For the heavens to extend into the earth, it must come through the atmosphere. In fact, when any spirit or spiritual thing—divine or demonic—seeks to extend its reach into the earth, its only port of entrance is either a human body or an open atmosphere. When God wants to do something in the earth, He either does it in the atmosphere or He does it through us. This is how God expands His world.

When He created the earth, He created it to exist as an extension of His world so that what happens in the heavens can also happen in the earth.

POWER IN THE AIR

What is an atmosphere? It's simply *power* that is felt and accessible in the air. It's really that simple, and Scripture backs this up in Ephesians 2:2. To understand this, we must embrace the reality that Ephesians 2:2 is speaking of more than merely sin and the devil. It is talking about the powers of the air, the governmental order of the spiritual world, and how its operations affect the world we live in. The only problem is that most theologians ignore this reality because it's talking about all of this in the context of the devil. Reducing the complexity of the supernatural world is very tempting to those who've read the Bible but have never experienced the supernatural or "power" for themselves.

However, if you think back to Chapter 3, you learned that the power that Ephesians 2:2 references did not originate with the devil. Instead, it originated with God, and how He structured His world like a kingdom. In other words, the devil did not create the demonic structure mentioned in Ephesians 2:2. The truth is that this highly sophisticated structure of spiritual rank existed among the angels. It still exists among the angels in heaven; the devil only mimicked it, but he could not create it because he isn't the creator. Therefore, we can look at this structure and understand how the heavenly world affects the world we live in. After all, this world is the world that Colossians 1:7 says was created by and for Christ Jesus, and yet exists in Christ Jesus.

Whenever something is making its transition from the supernatural world into our world, the power of it is felt in the atmosphere. The spiritual world then needs individuals to become aware of and cooperate with what is in the atmosphere for it to take up residence in the earth. This is the "power of the air." As Christians, we cooperate with this power through the power of the Holy Ghost. This is how we advance the Kingdom of God.

THE KINGDOM OF GOD

When Jesus explained the awareness of and the entrance into His Kingdom, He did so in the context of the wind. In other words, He did so in the context of the atmosphere. Why? Because this is the dimension of heaven that is directly accessible in the earth. The definition of the Kingdom of God is found in Matthew 6:10: "on earth as it is in heaven" (NKJV). The Kingdom of God is, in fact, an open heaven within the earth. Christians who understand this are beyond excited about going to heaven one day, but we are just as excited about bringing heaven down into earth.

Romans 15 teaches that the Kingdom of God is an

atmosphere in the Holy Ghost. This means that when we receive the Holy Spirit, we do not receive only a person but we also receive the backing of an entire Kingdom. In Luke 12, Jesus taught that the Kingdom of God is within us. When we show up, the Kingdom of God shows up with us. Its resources become our resources. Its laws become our laws. Its power becomes our power. It's literally called "the power of the world to come" in Hebrews 6:5. When Jesus entered a city, He always first announced that the Kingdom of God was at hand. He taught His disciples to do the same. This means that heaven is always near. I like to say that heaven is within arm's reach.

Do you see how expanded all of this actually is? Heaven is not just up, it's within, and it's always around us. This is the Kingdom of God—the reality of another world in our world through the power of God's Spirit.

THE KINGDOM AT HAND: OPEN HEAVENS AND CHANGING HEAVENS

What's happening in the atmosphere is connected to the reality of systems and operations of a more sophisticated world. The heavens that are over us and working in the atmosphere around us are determined by what spirit we entertain and allow in. Whatever we allow to dwell in us and dwell around us gains the influence. This is why we must be filled with Holy Spirit. This is also why demons seek the possession of our bodies. The spiritual world does not control our world. It only influences it. When spirits come into the earth, they do not come alone. Their objective is to extend their world into ours. This is God's primary objective in the earth. He wants His Kingdom in the earth as it is in heaven, and He accomplishes this through us. However, whatever spirit we allow in our space creates a spiritual place. This is how either the Kingdom of God or demonic principalities influence entire cities and nations.

My wife had an encounter of seeing two principalities. She describes one of them here:

One night my husband and I were praying with friends on the phone. We prayed very strongly in the Spirit. It was a glorious time of prayer, and a time that we knew that we had "broken through various forms of spiritual resistance." Before we got off the phone with our friend, he said, "Amanda, you're going to have a mighty encounter soon." I was very excited about it!

Not long after that phone call, while I was in my bed, I had an encounter. But I don't know if it was a dream or if I woke up and had a vision. It reminded me of when Paul said that "whether in the body or out of the body I do not know" (2 Corinthians 12:3 NKJV).

I saw a lady, who looked to be middle-aged, sitting in a chair. She seemed like a regular person in her appearance, but I could sense an evil presence around her. Her chair was suspended in the air and there were thousands upon thousands of people on the ground below her. From where she was seated, she began scanning the crowd, turning her head from the left to the right and back again as if she were searching for particular people that she could affect. She was seated in the second heavenlies, where the enemy is the prince of the air. I realized then that the woman was a principality.

In the vision, I was above the lady. She couldn't see me nor did she have any way of knowing that I was above her and could see her. The Bible says that we are seated in the heavenly places, and though I had read that Scripture for years, I had never understood until this vision that there are literally seats of authority in the heavenly places. That is the position where we want to be seated. We want to reside in the realm above where the enemy is.

We are not to be afraid of demonic forces; we are to live above them. It is a realm not known to the enemy, and we can ascend to that place. This is the access to and authority we have in the Kingdom of God.

What Jesus was establishing when He announced that His Kingdom had come was the same type of structure He was contending with when He entered certain territories. For every place represented in the earth, there is a spiritual place represented in its atmosphere, influencing its operations. This is why when you travel to different cities or nations, you can feel the difference in the atmosphere.

This was true of Daniel when dealing with the demonic principality that was influencing Persia. It was true of Jesus when He expelled the demons that had possessed the man at the tombs and who did not want to leave the region. It was also true of the power of sorcery that was in operation in the entire city of Samaria in Acts 8 prior to Philip's preaching the Kingdom of God there. The Scripture says specifically that Philip preached the Kingdom of God, and that is what changed the atmosphere of that entire city. The city went from being under a spellbinding curse to having joy, which is an attribute of a Kingdom atmosphere in the Holy Ghost, according to Romans 14:17.

What happened with Philip was no different from what happened with Jesus when He announced to entire cities and surrounding areas that His Kingdom had come. The heavens literally changed depending on how individuals responded to what came into their atmosphere in moments when the heavens had opened. This is what we call a shift. It is a noticeable difference in the atmosphere. It is a change in how powers and spiritual authorities are allowed to set up their rule in order to influence entire cities and nations.

When the Kingdom of God comes, the heavens do not just open; they change. Any demonic power influencing the atmosphere is displaced, and the rule of God is set up and reigns in the hearts of men through the Spirit of God.

WHAT THE PHARISEES DID NOT UNDERSTAND: ENTRANCE INTO GOD'S KINGDOM

The Kingdom of God is a powerful message, but it intimidated some of the leaders it came to help. Those who were greedy for power, whether religious or political, became very nervous at the announcement of the Kingdom, so much so that they wanted to get rid of Jesus. For the most part, the rulers of that day did not mind if Jesus healed the sick, cast out demons, or even raised the dead. However, they did not like the idea of Jesus announcing His Kingdom. They knew it meant that one government was seeking to overthrow another. They just didn't know it was a spiritual government. Therefore, the rulers literally interrogated Jesus on crimes against the government. Even though they did not understand the entirety of what Jesus was announcing, it still impacted their hearts in ways that drove them to jealously, rage, and eventually murder.

What if we regained the impact of this same message but with an understanding of its spiritual realities? If this message drove people to do evil things out of ignorance, how much more can it impact our lives for positive change? What if we learned how to cooperate with what God was doing and how He was moving supernaturally through His Kingdom? The impossible would become possible, and limits would be removed. But this happens only through the power of a Spirit-filled life.

This is what Jesus was trying to teach Nicodemus

in John 3. There, you see Jesus explaining the ways of the Spirit in the context of the atmosphere. He told Nicodemus that the only way Nicodemus could enter into how God's Kingdom was at work in the atmosphere around him was by the Spirit of God. We need to understand this too, if we are to fully interact with God and His supernatural world.

CHAPTER 5

THREE DIMENSIONS OF THE SPIRIT-FILLED LIFE

From the beginning of Jesus' ministry, there is a correlation between accessing the heavens and the ministry of the Holy Spirit. In Matthew 3:16, it was after the heavens opened that the Spirit of God descended on Jesus.

Jesus also made it very clear in John 3 that new life in the Holy Spirit is the only way to access the supernatural realities of God's world and Kingdom. The point is that the supernatural life is nothing less than and nothing contrary to a life full of the Spirit.

One of the biggest mistakes among Christians who embrace the supernatural is to become so focused on the realities of the supernatural world that we lose focus on the source of it all, which is a Holy Spirit–filled life. It's easy for those who appreciate the supernatural world to have their focus caught up in angels, open heavens, atmospheres, the invisible world, signs, wonders, etc.

The truth is that our ability to see the heavens at work around us is based on our ability to embrace the Kingdom within. Furthermore, it is through the Holy Spirit that we carry the Kingdom within. Remember, the Kingdom of God is in the Holy Ghost, according to Romans 14:17.

THE TRAGEDY OF TRADITION

The Scriptures teach a lot about the Spirit-filled life. However, what people learn in church is often reduced or watered down from what the Bible teaches.

The Holy Spirit is more than the power to live right or the power to become witnesses of Jesus, as seen in Acts 1:8. He is more than a helper, an advocate, and a divine advantage, as seen in John 14:16. He is more than one who convicts of sin and more than a revealer of truth, as seen in John 15:8–12. He is more than the giver of an ability to speak in tongues in order to help us pray to God, as seen in Acts 2:4 and 1 Corinthians 14:2. The Holy Spirit is more than the fruit of God's love and character that He develops in our lives, as seen in Galatians 5:18–22. He is also more than the gifts He distributes to help us serve in ministry more effectively, as seen in 1 Corinthians 12 and Romans 12. He is all these things and so much more.

The realities of the supernatural that are available to us are vastly beyond what I've mentioned so far. For example, the power of God's Spirit within us is literally called the powers of another world in Hebrews 6:5. Yet, even encountering that world in relation to the Spirit-filled life is not the only dynamic of the supernatural. The supernatural transformation we undergo as we embrace our identity in Christ is reliant upon the Spirit-filled life as well. Romans 8 teaches that our very identity is contingent upon our being led by the Spirit. In other words, the more you understand these things, the more you're going to walk in your inheritance and in your identity. The less you understand them, the more you're going to miss out. Understanding the fullness of the Spirit-filled life should be a priority in our pursuit of the supernatural. We cannot replace our pursuit of the Spirit with a lesser pursuit of encounters, angels, open heavens, and miracles. Everything we seek to know and experience of the supernatural is all made possible by the Holy Spirit. Therefore, we must increase our understanding of God's Spirit and various dynamics of the Spirit-filled life.

FOUNDATIONAL DYNAMICS OF THE SPIRIT-FILLED LIFE

The very first thing we should understand is that there are multiple dimensions to the Spirit-filled life that connect us to the reality of the supernatural. The Scriptures are extremely specific as to what aspect of the Spirit-filled life they are referencing in whatever given context.

For example, there is a difference between being "led by the Spirit" and being "filled by the Spirit." Being led by the spirit is talking about *power* whereas being "filled by the Spirit" is talking about *character*. Why? Because living in the Spirit is an ongoing progressive experience. It's not a once-in-a-lifetime event. Let's look at Ephesians 5:14 to understand this truth: *Be filled with the Spirit*. In the Greek, this isn't just an imperative. It's also in the perfect progressive tense. Therefore, the text is not merely speaking to someone who had never been filled with the Spirit. In the original language, the text is actually saying: *being filled continuously*. This rings true for how we ought to live. The reality is that if we are filled with the Spirit, it should be our goal to live in a perpetual state of being filled by the Spirit.

But the sad truth is that most Spirit-filled believers go through their Christian experience without experiencing fresh infillings. It's not that we "lose the Holy Spirit" or that He leaves us if we're not experiencing fresh infillings. But the truth is that something is wrong if we don't have a hunger and thirst for more. We should want more than a church encounter, more than a feel-good moment. The real issue is that we cannot be led by a Spirit we are not filled with.

It's not salvation that's at risk if not, but rather the

manifestation of the sons of God in the earth is what's at risk (Romans 8:19).

But once we are filled with the Spirit, we must learn how to live and function in the Spirit. And we will be active in things pertaining to the Spirit of God only to the measure that we allow Him to fill our lives.

THREE DIMENSIONS OF A SPIRIT-FILLED LIFE

There is a difference between a *sign* of having received the Holy Ghost and the *fruit* of living in the Spirit. They both come with the Spirit-filled life package, but they serve in different dimensions of it.

I'll be dissecting some of these truths to their core, truths we either often overlook or just overgeneralize. Why does this matter? Because ignorance of these truths cost us to lack seeing the Kingdom of God in full manifestation.

The sad reality is that there are many in the Body of Christ who are a part of a church congregation but have not been filled with the Holy Ghost. This means that many in the Body of Christ will not see the Kingdom. Why? Remember, we must be born or birthed into the Kingdom by the Spirit. Just as a baby stays in its mother's amniotic sac until its organs are fully developed, we, too, must stay in a place in the Spirit until we are developed enough that when we come out of the womb in the Spirit, we won't die. The goal is to come out of the womb of the Spirit healthy: hearing, breathing, eating, etc. The baptism of God's Spirit is that womb we are birthed into the supernatural out of.

When we hear teaching concerning our interaction with the Spirit of God communicated differently, we must understand that it is not merely a preference of words and articulation but rather a specific dimension of spiritual realities that the Scriptures are communicating.

The following three dimensions of the Spirit-filled life are great examples of this:

We are FILLED with the Spirit.
We are LED by the Spirit.
We then WALK in the Spirit that we are filled and led by.

The Scriptures detail distinguishable results that come through each dimension of the Spirit-filled life. Therefore, if we are misinformed concerning what the Scriptures say happens when an individual is *led* by the Spirit versus when an individual is *filled* with the spirit, we end up with a bunch of confused people. It shows in our teaching, and in the lifestyles of those who listen to the errant teaching. The reality is that just because an individual is filled by the Spirit doesn't mean they are being led by the Spirit they are filled with. Furthermore, if an individual never learns to be led by the Spirit, they'll likewise never walk in the Spirit they are filled with. This is key because each dimension only carries us more into the supernatural. The first dimension activates the power. The second dimension works on your character. The third dimension will have you operating in the supernatural.

First Dimension = POWER
Second Dimension = Character
Third Dimension = Fully Living and Operating in
the Supernatural

One of the reasons the church is full of people who are not mature in spiritual things is because we don't know how to monitor the proper growth that should be taking place in the Spirit. The levels of development are these: You are filled with the Spirit, then you are led by the Spirit, and then you walk in the Spirit. Spiritual development has nothing to do with how long an individual has been in ministry. It has nothing to do with how old an individual is. It has nothing to do with how much Scripture an individual thinks they know. Sadly, there are even leaders who are spiritual babies and don't realize it. How do we know? The proof is in the levels of illiteracy in the areas of the Spirit in which their spiritual development and growth are marked and measured.

This is partly what Jesus was dealing with concerning Nicodemus. Jesus knew Nicodemus was a spiritual leader and yet he did not know and could not comprehend some of the basic foundations of his spiritual livelihood, referenced in John 3. The apostle Paul had the same issue in Hebrews 5. His complaint against their church was that they should have been further along in their understanding of spiritual things after having been believers in Christ for so long. He then compared their ignorance to their spiritual maturity. What we learn is that no one ages in the Spirit by default. We must choose to grow up in the Lord and actively participate in the process.

The truth is that the part of our Christian experience in which we are filled with the Spirit is only where we are birthed in spiritual realities. It is not where we end, but where we begin. However, many have stopped there and are quite comfortable remaining there. It's the very reason why my wife and I are writing this book. We know that God is raising up a generation that wants all that He has for us. And we want to help everyone move from babyhood to full maturity in Christ.

THE FULL MEASURE OF THE SPIRIT

When it comes to measures in the Spirit, the Scriptures do not leave us in the dark. According to Ephesians 3:17–20, there is a full measure of the Spirit. There is a biblical way to measure what should be seen in an individual's life at specific stages of growth within their Spirit-filled walk. This is where the concept of "receiving the spirit with the evidence of speaking tongues" comes from. Each stage and each dimension of the Spirit-filled life has its own evidence, fruit, and benefits it makes available in a believer's life. If you prefer only certain aspects of the Spirit-filled life, you'll be inhibited in how your measure in the Spirit is increased.

If we're going to measure spiritual growth, we must begin at the beginning. The Scriptures give clarity on how to validate when a person has received the infilling of the Spirit. Pentecostals teach that you know a person is filled with the Spirit when they speak in tongues. Charismatics teach that you'll know a Spirit-filled believer by the character they develop. The reality is that both can tell you if a person is Spirit-filled, but each is representing a different stage of growth within the Spirit-filled life. Technically, the answer to the question "Are you filled with the Spirit?" can't be speaking in tongues and it also can't be developed character.

But if the question becomes more specific—as for example in Acts 19, "Have you received the Spirit since you've believed in Jesus?"—the answers can become more specific and detailed.

RECEIVING JESUS VERSUS RECEIVING AN INFILLING OF HIS SPIRIT

Receiving Jesus and receiving an infilling of the Spirit are two different encounters and experiences. We can't expect a person who has never received the infilling of the Spirit to live full of the Spirit. Living full of the Spirit is an ongoing encounter rather than a one-time experience.

Therefore, the infilling that takes place once an individual first receives the Spirit of God is only the initial infilling. This is the reason Ephesians 5 encourages us to live a life of ongoing infilling. I can't stress how key and foundational this is. However, every believer should distinctly know when they were originally filled with the Spirit and be aware when they experience successive fresh infillings. Acts 19:2–6; 8:14–17; 2:37–38; and 10:44–48 all establish that the infilling of the Spirit in a person was a separate experience from that individual first giving their life to Jesus. I want to warn you that this has become taboo in the Church. We have avoided these realities because of what they imply. And I'm afraid what's happening in the Church is that we are missing out on the fullness of the Spirit because we are afraid to suggest to people that they may not be Spirit-filled believers yet, although they may be saved already. Why does this matter? Because it is very easy to subscribe to cultural Christianity in which we know everything there is to know about attending church but not much about developing a viable relationship with God. The only remedy is we must be able to gauge where people are in the process and help guide them where they're headed in their spiritual growth. The only problem is that we can't do so with general, denominational, biased, opinionated, or just plain old uninformed suggestions of what it means to live the Spirit-filled life. We cannot have preferences in what we believe the Spirit-filled life should look like and then truly understand what that life is.

We must go deeper. We must have fresh infillings. There are people, not even saved yet, waiting to be born again who will need our discipleship and our maturity.

UNDERSTANDING THE THREE DIMENSIONS OF THE SPIRIT-FILLED LIFE HELPS TRACK SPIRITUAL GROWTH

If we are going to understand how Spirit-filled living is dimensional, we must begin with understanding that the Spirit-filled life is more than a Pentecostal experience. You can tell how limited an individual is in their understanding of the Spirit-filled life by how they answer the question of how they know when a person is filled with the Spirit. In the Body of Christ at large, the most common answers to knowing when a person is Spirit-filled are one of the following: speaking in tongues, receiving Jesus in your heart, living holy, having good character, or attaining spiritual gifts. However, the true Spirit-filled life is inclusive of all and exclusive of none of these. So, if I ask the question how I know if I'm filled with the Spirit, the answer depends on which dimension of the Spirit-filled life I'm referring to. It's only as we embrace the full measure of the Spirit-filled life that we can pinpoint what to expect within each stage of this life. In the process of doing so, we must begin thinking of the Spirit-filled life in terms of measures, stages, levels, and layers. The three basic growth progressions of the spiritual life are biblically described as follows: filled, led, walk. Therefore, the initial infilling of the Spirit is only the beginning of the Spirit-filled life. However, being filled with the Spirit is descriptive of both the initial and the constant growth in the Spirit scripturally.

The clarity is rooted in us understanding the difference between experiencing an infilling of the Spirit versus the call to live a life of constantly being filled with the Spirit. It may sound simple, but in most Pentecostal and charismatic streams, this is a major adjustment in our thinking. Among Pentecostal and charismatic circles, being filled with the Spirit is the destination, but in the Scripture, it is only the beginning of the journey (see Ephesians 5:18; Acts 2:4; 4:31). It is only as we understand these facts that we can also begin to understand the progression of growth in our spiritual life.

It is only as we thoroughly investigate the Scriptures that we notice that they don't speak generally but specifically of spiritual realities. The Spirit-filled life is not a one-size-fits-all. As we examine the Scriptures, we notice that for each dimension of the Spirit-filled life, there are different results associated with that dimension. This means that at every stage of our spiritual growth, we should be seeing different results. Remember that Ephesians 5:18 says, "Be filled with the Spirit." The text is telling us that our need to "be filled with the Spirit" is ongoing. The following two scriptural references are great examples of that truth: "...they were all *filled* with the Holy Ghost, and began to speak with other tongues" (Acts 2:4, emphasis mine). And: "...when they [the same individuals who were filled in Acts 2:4] had prayed, the place was shaken where they were assembled together; and they were all *filled* with the Holy Ghost" (Acts 4:31, emphasis mine). Notice: They were filled in Acts 2 and then they were filled again Acts 4.

Let's look again at the following chart. Feel free to refer back to it at any point for future reference:

Three Dimensions of a Spirit-Filled Life	
We are **FILLED** with the Spirit (Ephesians 5; Acts 2:4)	*Understanding and becoming more acclimated to the presence and power of God*
We are **LED** by the Spirit (Galatians 5:18)	*Becoming acclimated to the process of maturity = lifestyle: growing in capacity and character*
We then **WALK** in the Spirit we are led by	*Living in the supernatural; ultimately God wants to walk with you*

BEING FILLED WITH THE SPIRIT

The first dimension of a Spirit-filled Life is to be *filled* with the Spirit. According to the promise of God in Acts 1:8, which was fulfilled in Acts 2:4, you are to receive *power* when you are filled with the Spirit. The infilling of the Spirit is where the presence and power of God is accessed (Acts 1:8; 2:4). These are a sign to let us know when we have experienced an infilling of the Spirit. This is also where speaking in tongues come into play.

Many believe that when a person is filled with the Spirit, they should develop the fruit of the Spirit. This is error. The Scriptures do not reference the fruit of the Spirit to the infilling of the Spirit. The fruit of the Spirit is only in reference to the leading of the Spirit, which is a completely different dimension, but we will get to that later.

You have to understand that when Jesus promised power in reference to the infilling of the Spirit, Acts 1:8 records only a portion of that conversation with His disciples. We won't fully understand what was promised in Acts 1:8 and happened in Acts 2:4 unless we compare Mark 16:17–18; Luke 24:49; Matthew 28:18–19; Acts 1:8; and Acts 2:4 all together. They all feature different aspects of the same conversation that was taking place in Acts 1:4–8. More specifically, when Jesus promised power, the Mark 16:17 version of the conversation is most specific pertaining to the details of the power that was promised. As we read it, we will discover where speaking in tongues comes into the equation of being filled with the Spirit.

WHY SPEAK WITH OTHER TONGUES

In Mark 16:17 it says that *"these signs* shall follow them that believe, in my name shall they cast out devils; they shall speak with new tongues" (emphasis mine). The text clearly states that *signs* will follow us. This is significant because a sign is a demonstration of God's power. You must also remember that this is being promised in the context of the power of the Spirit that will come upon us. Therefore, the power we receive when we are filled with the Spirit is power to heal the sick, power to cast out demons, power for divine protection, and power to speak with other tongues. There are clearly multiple power dimensions promised to us. What's mentioned in Mark 16 is only foundational, but for now it's key in helping us build on this foundation.

Because of the diversity of power promised to us in being filled with the Spirit, we need to go deeper to understand why speaking in tongues is so important. There is a reason we see this manifestation so frequently as the sign that individuals had received the infilling of God's Spirit. I can give you just two biblical reasons that I believe will address this. The first reason that speaking in tongues was the key sign that individuals had initially been filled with the Spirit is because it was also the only power dimension they did not access before the cross. Therefore, speaking in tongues was the primary sign that an individual had been filled with the Spirit and had received the promise of power as a result.

And honestly, how else could the disciples have known that they had been filled with the Spirit if they were accessing only the same power they were able to access before the cross and resurrection of Jesus? There was something different about the promise of power that came with the Spirit. The second reason we know that speaking in tongues was important is because it was the only vertical expression of power. What do I mean by this? Every other dimension of power received by the disciples was horizontal in its expression. In other words, its purpose was to help other people. A vertical empowerment is how our personal relationship with God is empowered. Therefore, speaking in tongues is extremely significant. It is a vertical empowerment that keeps us connected to the Presence, where the power is sourced from. It is a new language given to us by which we can pray to God and not worry if we are praying correctly or even if our prayers are being heard, according to 1 Corinthians 14:2, 14.

The Scriptures speak of the phenomenon of speaking in tongues in more than one context. Therefore, what happened in Acts 2:4 when men first began to speak in tongues in the upper room is different from when an individual is operating in the gifts of the Spirit. One is vertical and one is horizontal. In other words, one ministers to God and the other ministers to men.

Therefore, the power promised with the infilling of the Spirit was not merely about the gifts of the Spirit. There are dimensions of power beyond the gifts that the Scriptures mention. This vertical type of unknown tongue is just one of many.

BEING LED BY THE SPIRIT

Being led by the Spirit is the second dimension of Spirit-filled living, and is where the fruit of the Spirit is produced, which is the reward of this dimension, according to Galatians 5:18–23.

It is in this dimension, and this dimension only, where we begin to become more like Jesus. Our character is developed as we learn how to be led by the Spirit. It's also the more excellent way of operating in the gifts of the Spirit according to 1 Corinthians 12:31. We know this because of what follows in the next chapter promises to show us a better way of accessing the gifts of the Spirit and directly correlates with the fruit of the Spirit mentioned in Galatians 5:18–23. This is a very profound reality. This is the reason why Elisha asked Elijah for a double portion of his spirit in his process of being mentored by him to be used of God powerfully. Therefore, Elisha knew that it was Elijah's personal integrity and character that determined the capacity in which God could use him. This is a mystery, because people without integrity can be used by God. However, they only go so far before they crash, and they never reach their maximum potential. This is what happened with King Saul.

In 1 Samuel 10, the Spirit of God came on Saul at the

time in which he had a good heart. He prophesied and was accurate. The prophecy was correct, and there were no problems. Then the Spirit of God came upon Saul a couple of chapters later, after he became rebellious and stubborn, and now there were problems. His heart had turned. The next time Saul prophesied, he did so while stripped naked. It was the same Holy Spirit on Saul, but because his heart had changed and his character had taken a turn for the worse, it was a bad experience.

Recently I attended some exclusive meetings with Pastor Benny Hinn and eight other pastors. He shared this reality as well. One of the things he told us that Oral Roberts taught him is that when the anointing of the Spirit comes on an individual, it stirs up everything in them, both the good and the bad. This is exactly what happened to Saul, and this is exactly what I've been learning about the difference between being filled and being led by the Spirit. If we do not allow the Holy Spirit to lead us in ways that result in the development of our character and integrity, the power of the anointing that comes on us due to the infilling of the Spirit will eventually cause the areas of our character that are underdeveloped to begin to show.

WALKING IN THE SPIRIT

Walking in the Spirit is where we learn to live in the supernatural. The reason we are led by the Spirit is so that we continue to walk in the Spirit that's leading us. Step by step, God will lead us along the way.

Walking in the Spirit is directly contingent upon the consistency in which we are led by the Spirit. This is one reason they, being led by and walking in the Spirit, are both mentioned in Galatians 5:16, 18. What we do know of walking in the Spirit is that if we do so, we will not fulfill the lust of the flesh, the love of God will be visible in our lives, and we will not live under the law. All great promises!

My favorite example of walking in the Spirit is Enoch. I love how Enoch lived in a supernatural dimension, to the same extent that he lived in the earth. The Scripture says he walked with God. How do you walk with God? You have to walk with Him in the spiritual dimension. This means that Enoch lived in two dimensions at the same time. This brings us back full circle to the reality of the Kingdom of God.

The truth is that the understanding of walking in the Spirit from Galatians 5:19 is rooted in the foundation of what Jesus distinguished between seeing and entering the Kingdom of God in John 3:3–5. They both reveal layers in the experience of spiritual realities. According to Galatians 5:19, just because we live in the Spirit does not mean we walk in the Spirit. Likewise, seeing and perceiving the Kingdom of God is completely different from entering or operating in the Kingdom of God.

In like manner, to be filled with the Spirit will not

suffice if we do not learn to walk in the Spirit that indwells us. Therefore, there are certain things we cannot avoid learning if we plan on fully accessing and operating in the supernatural. God does not want us to be aware of His Kingdom only. He wants us to operate and function in it.

In the next chapter, I'm going to begin cracking the code on certain secrets of the supernatural so that we can do just that. But first, I want to briefly bring clarity to a controversy that will free us to explore various spiritual realities without hesitation.

A FINAL OBSERVATION

I've noticed that many are offended with talk of the supernatural because of how, throughout church history, some of the men and women who moved in the supernatural eventually had moral failures. The offense is due to the lack of understanding of the three dimensions of the Spirit-filled life.

We can be filled with the Spirit but not surrendered to Him. Our spiritual life begins with being filled with the Spirit, but it does not end with being filled. This lack of understanding has caused many to be suspicious and believe that the supernatural is demonic. This is the very plan of the devil. The enemy's goal is for the church to reject our inheritance in Christ because of offense or fear.

The reality is that the Spirit-filled believer's walk progresses gradually throughout different levels of maturity. Everyone who has power does not necessarily have great character, and everyone who has character does not necessarily have the slightest grasp on everything that's available to them in God. We must treat this delicately. We must not reject the supernatural because of someone who operated in the supernatural outside of Godly maturity.

Not everyone is going to exhibit Godly maturity when dealing with the supernatural, which is why character is so important. Pursue a Godly character as you pursue the supernatural, and you will see the Spirit move in and through you in ways you've never imagined.

CHAPTER 6

CRACKING THE CODE

So if the Spirit-filled life is the entrance into the supernatural world, then praying in tongues is the engine of the Spirit-filled life. The phenomenon of speaking in "unknown tongues," as the Scriptures describe it, is a technology and even a weapon that helps us more proficiently navigate the supernatural dimension. Praying in tongues is like cracking a code that keeps the secrets of the supernatural concealed. It causes the mysteries of God to be unraveled and grants us access into dimensions of God's Kingdom that are quite mind blowing.

I'd literally been praying in tongues or had just finished praying in tongues when I had some of the most profound supernatural encounters. By the way, this is what John 3 is talking about when it mentions how we must be birthed in the Spirit to see and enter in the Kingdom. Seeing the Kingdom is a great joy and benefit, but entering the Kingdom is where we are literally walking in the Spirit like Enoch did. Entering the Kingdom is about interacting with God's world in the supernatural to the level of awareness and proficiency that you would in the natural world. Developing a discipline of praying in tongues can and will open the supernatural to you in ways you've never grasped before. Once you experience what I'm talking about, you'll never want to go back.

MY EXPERIENCE

Over these last ten years, I've prayed more in other tongues than I have in English, similar to what Paul experienced. In 1 Corinthians 14:18, he mentions that he prayed in tongues more than all the Church at Corinth. It's quite possible he prayed predominately in tongues. At bare minimum, we can suggest he prayed at least 50 percent of the time in tongues, according to 1 Corinthians 14:15. How could we suggest this? Because in this verse, he gives praying in the understanding and praying in the Spirit equal weight, which leaves us with a 50:50 ratio. I've personally found it to be more effective. I've also discovered it allows easy access into the supernatural.

Once, as I was praying in tongues, in a vision I literally saw a demonic authority thrown out of the sky into the ground. This means that my eyes were not closed.

I was very aware of all of my surroundings in the natural. I was outside at the time while praying, and I could see the trees and clouds. And then suddenly I saw the demonic power hurling down into the earth. It was the only spiritual thing I saw in this vision.

The very first time I saw a supernatural gateway open into the spiritual world was while I was praying in tongues. It literally looked like something from a Star Wars movie. Another time, directly after I was praying in tongues, I had an out-of-body encounter in which I went to heaven. On another occasion, while I was praying in tongues in my bedroom, I looked up and saw a heavenly creature standing directly in front of me whose body looked as if it were made of blue flames. I could go on and on, but I think you get the point. Praying in tongues is extremely powerful to understand the kinds of spiritual matters we've addressed so far.

SEVEN BENEFITS OF PRAYING IN TONGUES

1. We Increase Our Capacity for Manifestation

For he that speaketh in an unknown tongue speaketh not unto men, but unto God: for no man understandeth him; howbeit in the spirit he speaketh mysteries.

1 Corinthians 14:2

The Scriptures denote that when we speak in tongues, we speak in a mystery. A mystery is simply the hidden wisdom of God (2:7–10). It would take more than an eternity to even begin to conceive all the knowledge of God, because His ways are past finding out. God knows that there are things He wants to do that our lack of faith could possibly hinder. So, in turn, He gives us an unknown tongue to proclaim things that our minds don't have the capacity to understand in the natural (14:14). As we pray in this way, the hidden wisdom and revelation of God can be released in the Spirit. The mysteries of what God desires and plans to do are released in faith so that the manifestation has a landing strip—or way to enter the earth. As we proclaim the mysteries of God, we are preparing the way in the Spirit for the next thing God wants to do and open in our lives.

2. We Increase Our Capacity for Revelation

But we speak the wisdom of God in a mystery, even the hidden wisdom, which God ordained before the world unto our glory.

1 Corinthians 2:7

When exploring the subject of speaking in other tongues, there's a definite emphasis on the mysterious. However, what we should understand about a mystery is that it is not something that cannot be known. Rather, a mystery is something that can be made known only by way of revelation. In the same way, when we pray in tongues, we are praying things that can be made known only by revelation. This is important because where there is no revelation, there can be no manifestation. As we pray in tongues, those things that are a mystery to us in the natural are revealed to us in the Spirit. For example, there have been many occasions when my wife or I have been praying in tongues and have been given specific insight into various matters.

Furthermore, as we speak the mysteries of God in an unknown tongue, God opens revelation to us and causes the things of the Spirit to become more real to us than things in the natural. And as this takes place, the manifestation of what God wants to do in the earth can be accelerated. For example, there have been times when my eyes have caught glimpses of spiritual things that I couldn't make sense of or gain complete clarity of sight. This is what we find taking place in Job 4:14–16. The scriptural reference of the previous shows that sometimes we begin seeing in the Spirit, but what we are seeing is not yet clear. It has been in times like this that I have prayed in tongues and the revelation opens up more clearly to me.

What is Revelation?

Revelation is the processor of all divine communication and experience, as is shown in 1 Corinthians 2:9–11:

But as it is written, Eye hath not seen, nor ear heard, neither have entered into the heart of man, the things which God hath prepared for them that love him. But God hath revealed them unto us by his Spirit: for the Spirit searcheth all things, yea, the deep things of God. For what man knoweth the things of a man, save the spirit of man which is in him? even so the things of God knoweth no man, but the Spirit of God.

According to 1 Corinthians 2:7, a mystery is wisdom that has been hidden from our eyes, our ears, and our hearts. However, the good news is that the Spirit of God comes to reveal the things that have been hidden according. Therefore, 1 Corinthians 2:7–11, in its entirety, is teaching that when things (prepared for us by God) are revealed to us, they can be unraveled before our eyes, word of them will come into our ears, and they will be perceived in our hearts through the Spirit of God (2:9–11). In other words, revelation is not merely the understanding of a mystery but rather also what activates our ability to see, hear, and experience divine things that normally go undetected by our natural senses. This is the type of revelation that is available as we pray in tongues. You will find that dreams, visions, supernatural encounters, and other divine occurrences become the norm as you pray in this empowerment. In fact, this is what happened in Acts 2:1–4, the first time the Holy Spirit empowered the prayer life of the believers in the upper room. Not only did they speak in tongues, but they began to "see" in the Spirit tongues of fire, and they began to "hear" in the Spirit the sound of heaven, which was as a rushing wind. Likewise, as we pray in tongues, our capacity for revelation will be increased.

3. We Are Strengthened in Prayer

He that speaketh in an unknown tongue edifieth himself; but he that prophesieth edifieth the church.

1 Corinthians 14:4

Another thing that takes place as we pray in tongues according to the Scripture above is that we are edified. The word *edify* literally means to "build up and strengthen." This is important because our spirit man, which is the inner us, the most inner part of our tri-part being, is the incubator for what God wants to birth through our prayers (Ephesians 3:16–20).

In order to understand this, we must first understand that the Scripture teaches that the totality of who we are consists of spirit, soul, and body in 1 Thessalonians 5:23. This means we are tri-part beings. I explain more in number 6 of this chapter what it means for our spirit man to participate in our prayer efforts.

However, for now, it's key to recognize that our inner man, which is our spirit man, must be strengthened at times, according to Ephesians 3:16. More specifically, prayer is a key time in which our spirit man will need strength. When we are praying in our own strength, we have the tendency to "give in" before God "breaks in" and causes us to receive our "breakthrough."

Our spirit man must be strengthened and constantly built up so that we have the strength to "birth in prayer" without the labor of the birthing overwhelming us. A great example of this is seen when Elijah prayed for the abundance of rain. The Scriptures indicate that he prayed seven times with his head between his knees. This is significant because his position in prayer is historically known to be the birthing position of a Hebrew woman. The relevance here is that it takes endurance and stamina to prevail in this kind of prayer—no different from the endurance and stamina it takes for a woman to birth a child. Elijah was positioning himself in this manner to engage in a prophetic act that I believe God used to symbolically demonstrate what type of prayer is often required to birth a certain dimension of prayer.

At certain times, praying in tongues is the only way we will acquire the maximum momentum required in pressing a prayer through the birthing canal of the Spirit. Therefore, when we don't know what to pray or when we feel too weary to pray, that is the perfect time to pray in the Holy Ghost. As we first acknowledge our inability and inadequacy in prayer, there is a power activated in prayer that allows the Holy Ghost to strengthen our weaknesses and pray through us (Romans 8:15, 26).

4. We Pray at Maximum Potential

What is it then? I will pray with the spirit, and I will pray with the understanding also: I will sing with the spirit, and I will sing with the understanding also.

1 Corinthians 14:15

In this Scripture, when Paul speaks of praying in the understanding, he is speaking of praying in our native tongue. This means that when we pray only in our native tongue, it means that our prayer can never exceed beyond what we do or do not understand. Therefore, if there is no change after we have done all we know to do in prayer, it is evident that we don't know all there is to know or be done in prayer.

When praying in our native tongue, it's easier to pray below our maximum potential or to even pray amiss because we can pray only to the extent of our knowledge, which is limited. The problem is that our faith will never exceed our understanding. However, when we pray in the Holy Ghost, we pray beyond our rationale. We pray beyond our intellect. We pray beyond our mental blocks. We pray even above our comprehension. When we pray in the Spirit, we pray beyond the personal limitations we have set on ourselves and the limitations we've allowed others to set on us. In the Spirit, we pray beyond our inner conflicts and beyond the limitations of even our greatest dreams. There is a power that can be activated within us as we pray that gives God the permission to perform in our lives beyond anything we can imagine (Ephesians 3:20). There is a maximum potential we can reach in prayer only as we pray in tongues.

5. We Access Supernatural Faith

But ye, beloved, building up yourselves on your most holy faith, praying in the Holy Ghost.

Jude 20

Here, Jude 20 is stating that we are built up as our holy faith is built up. It also teaches us that this takes place as we are praying in the Holy Ghost. In other words, as we pray in the Holy Ghost, our holy faith is built up. And as our holy faith is built up, we are built up. Therefore, understanding our holy faith is the key to understanding the benefits of praying in the Holy Ghost.

The word *holy* means "separate, distinguished, and other than." Therefore, our holy faith is faith that is distinct from our *measure of faith* (Romans 12:3). Let me explain. The measure of faith is the level of faith that any one of us walks in at any given moment. This is the only type of faith that the Scriptures mention we have stewardship over. We are the ones responsible for whether our measure of faith is decreased or increased. This means that our faith levels are different depending on the circumstances. At times, our faith can be small, and at other times, our faith can be great. But the good news is that even in times when our faith is small, God has empowered us to be able to access faith beyond our personal measure of faith. That is holy faith in the Holy Ghost, which we access supernaturally as we pray in tongues.

The following Scripture references show great examples of holy faith:

When Jesus saw their faith, he said unto the sick of the palsy, Son, thy sins be forgiven thee.

Mark 2:5

This Scripture is a portion from the story about a man with palsy who was then forgiven and healed by Jesus. The Scriptures say that Jesus saw "their faith," which, according to the text, is not only in reference to the faith of the man with the palsy but also the faith of his friends with him. This means that the faith Jesus saw had a lot to do with the faith of the friends who brought the man with palsy to be healed—the faith of the man with palsy was not the only faith in operation when he was healed. It was the faith of his friends, which was faith that was "distinct" from his own faith. This is very symbolic of holy faith because it is representative of faith that comes from a source completely separate from our own measure of faith.

The revelation here is that when we in and of ourselves don't have the faith that God requires, there is yet another faith that we can access by the Holy Ghost, if we will pray in tongues. Now before you think that I have stretched my theology, let's look at the following text as another example of holy faith.

And straightway the father of the child cried out, and said with tears, Lord, I believe; help thou mine unbelief.

Mark 9:24

Here, notice the father's statement in the text, "I believe; help thou mine unbelief." He was basically saying to Jesus that "part of me is in doubt while part of me is accessing another source of faith." I believe that the father accessed the faith that was in Jesus Christ despite his tendency to hold on to his own doubt.

Holy faith is the faith that our doubt cannot cancel out. Even when our minds start to doubt or waiver, if we learn how to start praying in the Holy Ghost, there is a faith that will build our spirits back up. This is the holy faith in the Holy Ghost that we build as we pray in tongues. In fact, the word *building* in Jude 20 literally means to "supercharge." This means that when we pray in tongues, not only do we build our faith, but more specifically we literally supercharge our holy faith. There is power working inside us that, when activated, can perform beyond our highest thoughts and our utmost prayers: "Now unto him that is able to do exceeding abundantly above all that we ask or think, according to the power that worketh in us" (Ephesians 3:20).

6. Our Spirits Pray

For if I pray in an unknown tongue, my spirit prayeth, but my understanding is unfruitful.

1 Corinthians 14:14

When we pray in tongues, our spirits pray. This is significant in that our spirits are the core of who we are. If our spirits are praying, then it means the "real us" is praying when we pray in tongues, and we are literally praying out of our spirit man. This is key, because there are times when God makes certain deposits within us that we can't necessarily articulate. But when we pray in the Spirit, it is a surefire way to see to it that what has been deposited within makes its way out of us.

There are things within us that God wants to mature, things that He wants to have expressions of in the earth. These things must be cultivated. The gifts inside us must be stirred. And praying in tongues is a necessary way to develop the unique qualities God has placed within our spirits.

7. We Pray the Perfect Will of God

Likewise the Spirit also helpeth our infirmities: for we know not what we should pray for as we ought: but the

Spirit itself maketh intercession for us with groanings which cannot be uttered. And he that searcheth the hearts knoweth what is the mind of the Spirit, because he maketh intercession for the saints according to the will of God. And we know that all things work together for good to them that love God, to them who are the called according to his purpose

Romans 8:26–28

Technically Romans 8:26–28 is not talking about praying in tongues. We know this because it clearly says that these prayers are without utterance, which disqualifies all languages. However, the benefits of this type of Spirit-empowered prayer can be applied to speaking in tongues. This is true because of how we understand praying in tongues to be referenced scripturally, as both praying out of our spirits and praying in the Holy Ghost. This is possible because of how the Holy Ghost is infused into and one with our spirits (1 Corinthians 6:17). Therefore, although the truths in Romans 8:26–28 apply when speaking in tongues, they are not limited to speaking in tongues. The truth is that there is a union between our spirit and the Holy Spirit. Because of this, there are times when our spirits take the driver's seat when praying in the Spirit and other times when the Holy Spirit takes control. This is why we are called to "pray in the Holy Ghost" just as much as we are called to allow "the Holy Ghost to pray in and through us." They are two different functions that activate the same power in prayer. This is a mystery.

It is clear through Scripture that the Holy Ghost can pray through us in another language, yet it's equally clear that the Holy Ghost can pray through us, perfectly interceding for us through groanings that we cannot put into words (Roman 8:27). When we make the decision to pray in tongues, our spirit is leading the efforts in prayer by way of our own choice (1 Corinthians 14:14). There are also times when the Holy Ghost initiates the intercession and causes us to begin to pray in other tongues. However, He can, at times, take over in prayer in ways we cannot verbalize.

Above all else, praying in the Holy Ghost will cause us to walk in God's will. In fact, it is in the context of this Spirit-empowered intercession that all things work together for our good (Romans 8:27–28). Holy Spirit–empowered prayer always intervenes for us in ways that implement God's perfect will for our lives. Therefore, when dealing with the supernatural, praying in the Holy Ghost can prove to be of utmost importance. It can establish safeguards around our heart against spiritual error and fascination that attempt to draw us out of God's will. A strong prayer life will also keep our focus on Jesus, and not on various spiritual trends that can lead to deception.

As we embrace a lifestyle of praying in tongues, it will increase our capacity to comprehend and experience various dimensions of God in the supernatural. Why would anyone deny this empowerment? Praying in tongues will strengthen our spirits and add endurance to our prayer life. It will give us the stamina we need to increase our breakthrough capacity in prayer while most of all centering us in the perfect will of God.

A foundation of prayer is essential for anyone who's hungry to explore the supernatural. In fact, it's impossible to comprehend the depths of the Spirit without stability and consistency in prayer. The Scriptures teach that as we seek the Lord in prayer, He will answer us and show us great and mighty things that we are yet to understand (Jeremiah 33:3). The practice of prayer is a sure way to connect God's "super" to our "natural."

CHAPTER 7

SEEING AND ENTERING
THE KINGDOM

Up to now, we've talked about the necessity of a Spirit-filled life in dealing with the supernatural world. We know we cannot see or enter the supernatural world unless we are birthed into that world by the Spirit of God. What's next? We need to conduct an examination of what our entrance into that world looks like. Through Joel 2 and Acts 2:17, we discover that as the Spirit of God comes on us, we begin to experience dreams and visions. This is key, because dreams and visions are the reality of what it means to seeing the Kingdom of God in a literal sense of engaging the supernatural. They are how we navigate the spiritual world. In other words, if we understand the dynamics of vision and spiritual encounters, we gain context in understanding what Jesus meant by seeing and entering the Kingdom of God, and we will discover the power of our spiritual sight.

WHAT IS SPIRITUAL SIGHT?

Spiritual sight primarily deals with dreams and visions. However, for definitive purposes, I will examine visions, because the words "vision" and "dream" are the same word in the Hebraic and in the Greek. However, I'll sum up the difference between the two briefly before continuing. The difference between a dream and a vision is the level of symbolism that is utilized in the experience of both. Dreams are often parabolic and metaphoric in nature. Therefore, they require interpretation. On the contrary, visions tend to be more direct.

Yes, there are times when visions require interpretation. However, in the Scriptures we only see visions that require interpretation in times in which the visions are pertaining to the last days. At other times, visions are more precise and targeted to directly and plainly communicate an intended message. The life of Daniel is a great example of this. In the very beginning of Daniel's career as a politician, the king he served under had a troubling dream that he could not interpret. It bothered the king so much that he threatened to sentence the Cabinet that Daniel served on to death if they could not tell him the meaning of the dream. Of course, Daniel didn't want to die, so he prayed before falling asleep that God would show him the meaning of the dream. God did just what Daniel asked. However, the way in which God answered Daniel is significant in order to understand what I'm talking about concerning the difference between dreams and visions.

The Scripture says that when Daniel went to sleep, God gave him a "night vision" to answer him about the meaning of the king's dream. The Scripture is specific in this matter for a reason. Although Daniel was asleep when he saw what he saw, God did not classify what he saw as a dream. The reason was that if God had given Daniel a dream, Daniel then would have needed an interpretation of the dream he had seen. Therefore, God gave Daniel a vision in the night. It was in the vision that Daniel was informed of both what the king had dreamed and what the meaning of the dream was.

Powerful, isn't it? Dreams and visions both require you to see, but they can operate completely differently. I call this the seer's dimension. I categorize it as such because it deals with spiritual sight on multiple levels. This is where it really gets good.

THREE LEVELS OF SPIRITUAL SIGHT/VISIONS

There are seven different Hebraic words for the one English word, "vision." All seven of those definitions can be combined into just three categories, which ultimately represent three levels of spiritual sight. They are inward sight, open visions, and vision encounters. I call this the seer's dimension.

Inward Sight

The first level is *inward sight*. Many classify this dimension of sight as inner visions or closed visions. This level of sight takes place predominantly in your thoughts or your imagination. It's not to be overlooked, because it becomes the bridge into the next level of sight.

A lot of your inner vision has to do with impressions upon your spirit or glimpses that take place in your mind. We often call them daydreams. Most important, an inner vision deals with your imagination. Remember, the Scriptures do not teach that our imaginations are evil or fake. The imagination is of God. Therefore, Ephesians 1:18 teaches that God desires to enlighten the eyes of your imagination.

Now the English word used there is "understanding." We read the text as "the eyes of your understanding," but the Greek word for that is not understanding, it's "imagination."

The imagination is where your spiritual eyes exist. Therefore, the first level of being able to see in the Spirit has everything to do with you engaging your imagination. Again, does this mean what you're seeing is fake?

No. When I see angels or angelic activity, I see them like I see anything else.

The truth is that if you do not embrace your imagination, it could hinder your ability to see in another level as well. The imagination is more real than what we think is real. It is the potential of the spirit world. In other words, your imagination sees only glimpses of what already is, so that you can summon those things in the earth. This is the principle understanding of Romans 4:17: "God, who gives life to the dead and calls those things which do not exist as though they did." This speaks of how we call things into existence in our world. The reality is, if it's not in our world, but we want it in our world, all we must do is call it in. The hidden key in this verse, however, is that we are not to call things into existence as if we want them to come into existence, but rather as if they already were in existence. "Were" is the key term in the text. Notice, the things that we call into existence in the text are mentioned in past tense. Basically, everything that comes to this earth already existed in another world. However, they only transition from one world into our world by how we call them into our world. That's the power of your imagination. It gives you a glimpse into the spiritual world so you can hope for something, work toward something, move toward something, pursue, and push toward something in this world.

Open Visions

The second level of spiritual sight is classified as *open visions*. This is basically when you see in the Spirit, so that you could see me as if I were standing right in front of you. There's no other explanation, but that you see it. It's not your imagination, and it's not your mirage; you see it with your own eyes. However, it's not your natural eyes seeing it; it's your spiritual sight. This level of sight links us directly to one of the primary of the seven definitions for the word *vision*. One of these words is "looking glasses." It's almost as if heaven puts a pair of supernatural prescription glasses on your face so that you can see what would normally be invisible to you. Although you will see clearly, you're yet seeing in increments. Open vision often opens gradually. This means that when someone finally sees a full interactive type of vision with panoramic view, they have often come into different levels of spiritual activity leading up to that point that they may or may not have been aware of. Normally, you have *awareness*, and then you have *interaction*. Yes, sometimes seeing begins with simply an awareness of spiritual activity. Just like in the natural, your spiritual vision has a peripheral view. In other words, you don't see clearly what you do not focus on. It's no different from what you'd see if a car was passing by the window of your home while you were reading a book, or a fly flew directly across your face. We often see those things, but we don't make out the full form because they're simply not our focus. The Lord showed me that our spiritual sight works the same way.

This reality could provide an explanation to what happened in 2 Kings 6. Here, we see the prophet Elisha asking the Lord to open the eyes of his servant. In the natural, his servant's eyes were already opened. Therefore, Elisha wasn't referencing his servant's natural eyes in the prayer, but rather his servant's spiritual eyes. When God opened his eyes, he could see in the Spirit with just as much clarity as he could see in the natural.

I predominately see in this dimension, and so does my wife. When I mention that I've seen something in the Spirit, I have not seen it in my mind or imagination. I see what I see in the Spirit predominately with the same clarity as I see the natural world around me. This is the reason why Hebrews 5:13 encourages us to develop our spiritual senses, so that we can see clearly in many different ways.

Second Peter 1:19 is a great explanation of how visions gradually open: "...you do well to heed as a light that shines in a dark place, until the day dawns and the morningstar rises in your hearts" (NKJV).

Open visions begin when you have an awareness of supernatural activity. However, it's not until you acknowledge this that you have interaction and clarity of sight. Furthermore, the clarity of sight normally comes in one or two ways. The first is through panoramic sight. Vivid is an understatement. It's almost as if everything in the natural disappears and what exists in the Spirit dominates your sight during the duration of the vision.

But remember, open visions don't begin like this. Just in case this reality may intimidate you, you must understand that everyone has this capacity of sight. But it may begin with an awareness of activity and not full clarity of sight. The movement is similar to how your eye would catch a shadow, but it's not darkness. There are times you may see what literally looks like shooting stars flying around in the air around you. You may randomly see a sparkle. Sometimes it's like the air is literally moving or vibrating. What do I mean by vibrating? The outline of an angel's body often resembles heat waves coming off a car on a hot day. It's like seeing a human shape of vibrating air in your living room. At other times, you may see a flash. Or you may see something go by you quickly. That's often the activity that precedes the entrance into a vision. It's represents the truth that you are beginning to interact with the supernatural dimension. This is why you can't believe that your mind or eyes are playing tricks on you. Because the more you begin to focus, the more the vision will go from activity into panoramic view or clarity of sight.

And if you find yourself focusing on what you've begun to notice, the vision will open more. That's what happened to Peter in Acts 11. And it's what happened in Exodus 3 with Moses. The more they focused on what God was showing them, the more God opened the vision and showed them more.

You see, vision may start seemingly small, more like the light of a candle in a dark place. However, the more you engage it, the more its brightness shines more like the brightness of the sun. Sometimes the vision is panoramic. Other times the vision is layered with your natural sight. This is the second type of clarity that I want to cover. In this level of sight, you are seeing two worlds simultaneously. For example, if you were outside, you would still see the trees, mountains, or landmarks, but you'd also see the angels. You see in the natural and the spiritual at the same time. I have seen portals open while driving my car, and it did not distract my driving. I've also seen portals open right in my bedroom. It's like the air opens and I see into the supernatural, but at the same time I see everything in my room. I've also seen "invisible" people, where I could see the outline or a translucent figure of a person.

Just in case you're wondering, "What if it's demonic?"—you must understand that this level of sight is how the spiritual gift, *discerning of spirits*, operates. The word *discern* in 1 Corinthians 12 means "to see." This means that if you have not seen anything, you have not discerned anything. True and biblical discernment is not negative or suspicious. It is a type of spiritual sight. Therefore, when you begin to see and become aware of supernatural activity, that sight comes packaged with discernment by default. You will automatically know if it's demonic or angelic. After that point, the only other thing it needs to be examined by is the Word of God.

Open visions begin with an awareness, knowing that

the supernatural dimension is ever present by faith. It's about knowing that the heavens are constantly open. Once you believe that the heavens are always open to us by the Spirit of God, you will begin to see the activity of that very reality.

Let's look at the life of Daniel to gain more clarity in this phenomenon. Daniel 8:1 says, "In the third year of the reign of king Belshazzar a vision appeared unto me," and Daniel 10:7 says, "And I Daniel alone saw the vision." Here, Daniel is explaining two totally different experiences in which he had seen a vision. But our understanding comes when we realize that there are two different Hebraic words being used in the two texts. This is an example of what I meant earlier when I mentioned that there are seven different Hebraic words represented by the one English word, "vision." Therefore, Daniel is dealing with two different levels of sight in the two texts. More specifically, the level of sight in the vision of Daniel 8 was an inward sight. However, the level of sight in the vision of Daniel 10 was obviously an open vision.

Daniel is one of my favorite examples of how we see in different levels. The key I've learned in all of this is that there is often a progression in our spiritual sight as we honor whatever level of sight God allows us to see in predominantly. In other words, if you want to see more clearly, you must first acknowledge and respect the level you are already seeing in. You can't allow someone else's ability to see in the Spirit intimidate or discourage you from seeing how God wants you to see.

Most of the time when I see features, colors, or full-form, I'm in a trance or I'm out of my body. But most of the time I'm mostly seeing activity. For example, if I'm seeing an angel, I can often see the shape, I can see the height, and I know it's huge. Or I see the power glowing around the angel in a human form. When my wife sees in the Spirit, it's almost always panoramic, and she's able to see all sorts of vivid details. For example, when she sees, she sees the nose shape, the eye color, the hair, what color of clothes the angel has on, etc. Once, she had a detailed vision of the White House and why God did not want a certain individual to win the presidential election. It was full of specific and incredible detail. Honestly, the experience seemed foreign to me because she was seeing in the Spirit, but I was not at that moment. She mentioned how in the vision the Lord assigned her to pray for those in the White House.

I wasn't sure how to take it or how to respond until what happened next. The very next day we received an invitation to attend a faith-based initiative meeting at the White House. It was totally unexpected. Obviously, her prayers were effective.

And what would have happened had I not honored what she was seeing in the Spirit? I've learned not to be impulsive in how I respond to spiritual matters that I do not completely understand. It's important to me that I'm not dismissive to revelation that my wife or anyone else has that I may not possess. No matter how much we understand in the supernatural, we still have to remain in a position of trust and humility. We don't compete with each other's level of sight; we honor them. This is how you must be in your own life. The point is, the more you acknowledge the activity and honor it, the more you sharpen your own sight.

Vision Encounters

The third level of sight is a *vision encounter*. I love this level because it's excitingly different from open visions. In a vision encounter, you enter the vision. It's like supernatural virtual reality. In this level of spiritual sight, you are engaging the supernatural dimension with all your sensory capabilities and not just your sight.

This reality shows the greater significance of spiritual sight. The truth is, your spiritual sight is your dominant sense. For example, the word *see* in the Hebraic means "to experience with all your senses." Sight is not dealing with just seeing but encountering the supernatural world. It's not merely a vision. There's a level of a vision you can go into where all your senses will be activated.

THE CONNECTIVITY OF OUR SPIRITUAL SENSES

To understand how our spiritual sight is the dominant spiritual sense, you must first understand the connectivity of our spiritual senses. Habakkuk 2:1 is a great illustration of such: "I will stand upon my watch...to see what [the Lord] will say unto me." The key to understanding what I'm about to share is understanding that Habakkuk was a seer prophet. In other words, the prophetic anointing on his life had an emphasis on his ability to see in the Spirit. This means that Habakkuk would have more of a tendency to see or experience a vision encounter rather than merely hearing the voice of God if God was communicating with him prophetically. This is exactly what's taking place in the text.

With that in mind, notice how Habakkuk details that he's rather going to hear God through his eye and not through his ear. How? He's going to see what the Lord will say because his ear was connected to his eye.

This is the connectivity of our spiritual senses. And this is what Habakkuk was experiencing when he mentioned that he would see what the Lord would say. He understood that in a vision his hearing was connected to his sight, his sight was connected to his taste, his taste was connected to his smell, and his smell was connected to his touch. This is what the Psalmist was saying in Psalms 34 when he invited us to taste and see that the Lord is good. Basically, he's saying, "Oh, experience with all your senses and know with all your being that the Lord is good."

That's why Jesus said when an individual is praying, and finds somebody to agree with, it is as if you are touching what you are asking for (Matthew 18:19). Why? Because your mouth has a hand in it. Your taste is connected to your touch. Proverbs teaches that life and death are in the power of the tongue. The word *power* in the Hebraic is the same word for "hand." So, if your mouth has a hand in it, when you speak things, you're not just saying words, but you're touching the things that you're saying in the realm of the Spirit. In the Spirit, all your senses are connected. This is how one experience leads to another when in a vision because your sight is your dominant sense. Therefore, in a vision, all your senses can be activated, which is what distinguishes between merely seeing a vision and entering the vision.

This is what happened with Ezekiel. He was in a vision when he then conversed with an angel, which involved two senses, sight and hearing. Then the angel that he conversed with handed him a scroll, which now means his sense of sight, hearing, and touch are active, but it does not end there. The angel that handed him the scroll then instructed him to eat the scroll, after which Ezekiel noticed the scroll was sweet to his taste, which means that Ezekiel's sight, hearing, touch, and taste sensory capabilities were all active within this one vision. Ezekiel was not merely seeing this vision, he was in the vision. Furthermore, there were multiple times that either angels or the Spirit of God would literally come to Ezekiel, grab him, and carry him away into visions. The Scriptures even reported how Ezekiel would feel various sensations of traveling and being transported within these vision encounters. This is no different from what

I referenced experiencing earlier in the book, and what Paul mentioned in 2 Corinthians 12:1–4.

However, when it reaches this point, the encounter is more so a trance or an out-of-body experience. Trances are not mentioned much in the Scriptures but they are there. They can be defined, by examination of Acts 11, as a state that an individual goes into experience a vision. These types of vision encounters require a full range of motion, which is something that our spiritual sight triggers. In this level of supernatural activity, a vision can literally become a vehicle of transportation. This explains how Elisha, in 2 Kings, caught his servant receiving gifts from the king that he commanded him not to receive. He informed his servant that his spirit had gone with him. This means he traveled to the place by the Spirit of God to see what he needed to see.

Paul did the same thing in the New Testament when God caused him to be present in spirit where the Church he led was gathered, although his physical body was in another location. He could debrief the Church about specific things that were taking place. He, too, informed his correspondents that he was literally beholding and watching their order in the Spirit. Basically, he was saying he could see what they were doing. The progression of sight here was that he went from seeing a vision to going in the vision; and because he was in the vision, he had access to specific places in which the vision was giving him sight into.

Elijah could see certain things in different locations.

Ezekiel could see certain things in different locations. The apostle Paul could see certain things in different locations. Jesus did, too, as shown in John 1:48–50 (my paraphrase). The first thing that Jesus said when he met Nathaniel was, "I saw you in the location you were in before Philip brought you out to meet me." Jesus basically said, "I saw you before Philip saw you." Of course, Nathaniel was impressed by this, but Jesus went further and said, "If you think the prophetic is something, brace yourself, because you're going to see greater things than this." Jesus told Nathaniel that he would see the heavens open and see the angels going in and out of heaven, assisting Jesus in His ministry.

There's something deeper here than the prophetic and hearing from God. The realities of heaven exist around us all the time. Therefore, the Holy Spirit is not just how God interacts with us in our world, but also how we interact with God in His. For this to take place, we need our senses active. When this happens, our spiritual sight and the activation of our spiritual senses give us full mobility to operate and function in the supernatural world. Everything you can do in the natural you can do in a vision encounter.

CHAPTER 8

THE ACTIVATION OF OUR SPIRITUAL SENSES

More than we know, Scripture has a lot to say about our spiritual senses, and Hebrews 5:14 is just one example, saying that strong meat (or solid food) belongs to those who are mature, who have their senses exercised. The reality is that we need our spiritual senses to operate in the spiritual world, in the same way that we need our natural senses to operate in the natural world.

Can you imagine living in this world without your five natural senses? Unfortunately, there are some who do. It's not normal or preferred. In fact, it's called a handicap. Likewise, it's very possible to be handicapped in our attempt to engage the spiritual world. Which is why I've put great emphasis on exercising our spiritual senses in this chapter. It will help us avoid the danger of lacking in our ability to interact with God's Kingdom on earth.

TWO ELEMENTS THAT ACTIVATE OUR SPIRITUAL SENSES

2 Corinthians 5:7 states, "For we walk by faith, not by sight." This Scripture shows how faith is the first element that activates our spiritual senses. But what does it mean to walk by faith and not by sight? The answer is in the definition of the word *sight*, which in the Greek means not just one's ability to see, but rather focusing more on one's sensory capability, consisting of the five natural senses. Therefore, the Scripture is saying that we walk by faith, not by our natural senses. More specifically, 2 Corinthians 5 is dealing with our spiritual senses in contrast to our natural senses. It is talking about faith in the context of our spiritual sight, as does Habakkuk 2. The reality is that there is correlation in the seer's dimension and how faith is intertwined with the supernatural. In fact, faith is impossible without the supernatural.

Faith is not merely believing in something you cannot see. Hebrews 11:1 is the only Scripture in the Bible that attempts a verbatim definition of faith: "Now faith is the substance of things hoped for, the evidence of things not seen." Everything about it shouts, "Supernatural!" In this passage it is extremely clear that faith is the substance of *things*. But not just any thing. More specifically, it is the evidence of things unseen. In other words, faith takes something that is intangible and makes it tangible. Faith takes something that is invisible and makes it visible. Which brings us back to one of the primary principles we learned about supernatural realities in Chapter 3. Remember, invisible doesn't mean you cannot see it. Invisible means that you do not see it *yet*.

This is where it gets profound. Remember, the truth of walking by faith is found in 2 Corinthians 5:7 and written in context of 2 Corinthians 4:17, which teaches us that we can see the invisible. Therefore, when we properly link these two verses, as originally intended, the Scripture is actually teaching us that we can see while also telling us how to see in the same conversation. The only issue is that we just need to learn how to see. This is the power of faith. The truth is that 2 Corinthians 5:7 has an often-unnoticed correlation with Hebrews 5:14. One Scripture is saying we do not walk by our senses, and the other is saying our senses need to be exercised. Why? Because one is talking about our natural senses and the other, our spiritual senses. Faith is how our spiritual senses are activated. And 2 Corinthians 5:7 has a lot to say about living as if we're aware of the other world through our spiritual sight versus being limited to what's in the natural world by our natural sight.

The second element that activates our spiritual senses is our spiritual sight. Spiritual sight is key because of all our spiritual senses, spiritual sight is the most dominant for this simple reason. It triggers the activation of all of our other spiritual senses. We know this, because one of the definitions for the word *see* in the Hebraic tongue is "to experience with all your senses." This is how it was within a vision. Many of the prophets of the Old

Testament as well as the apostles of the New Testament had full interaction in a vision with the spiritual world through the activation of their spiritual senses.

It's really that simple. The more we see into the supernatural, the more it activates our full spiritual capacity over time. Visions are the vehicles in which we interact and fully operate in the spiritual dimension. This requires the activation of our spiritual senses. However, this only makes sense as we understand that our spiritual senses are only a portion of our spiritual anatomy just as our natural senses are only a portion of our natural anatomy.

THE SPIRITUAL ANATOMY

In 1 Corinthians 15:44, we see we don't just have spiritual senses but that we have a spiritual body:

There is a natural body, and there is a spiritual body.

And so, if we have a spiritual body, we also have spiritual anatomy. Our spiritual senses are merely part of our spiritual anatomy. Just think, if a scientist is still trying to figure out our natural body's anatomy and still hasn't accomplished it, how much more complex must our spiritual anatomy be? Though this reality is weighty, it's also simply true that if you can see in the natural, if you can hear in the natural, if you can touch in the natural, if you can smell in the natural, if you can taste in the natural, you can also do that in the Spirit. This is why there are plenty of examples of prophets and apostles fully engaging the supernatural world through a vision in which they had full spiritual sensory capability. It was in a vision that Ezekiel tasted a scroll. Furthermore, the scroll had a sweet taste, and beyond that, it made his stomach bitter. He also experienced a vision in which he felt the sensation of being carried away to various locations; he felt the emotional pull of God's heart toward certain situations, saw angels, and engaged in dialogue with some of the messengers sent to him by God. He had full spiritual sensory capabilities.

RECOVERING THE SEER'S DIMENSION: WHEN THE PROPHETIC IS OVERRATED

The subject of spiritual sight is often overlooked because in the prophetic there is a focus usually only on one of our senses. Too often the other four senses go ignored. It's a travesty that we are training an entire generation to hear God, activate, and prophesy without realizing that we are still raising handicapped Christians if that's all we are doing. An ability to hear God is not true proficiency in the prophetic, because there are so many ways that God interacts with us.

You can be given understanding through the silence of God, just as much as you can get understanding when

God speaks. Why? Because the supernatural extends so far beyond hearing the voice of God. In fact, the seer's dimension, the three levels of spiritual sight discussed in Chapter 7, was the primary way that God interacted with His people in Scripture: God communicated primarily in either a dream or a vision.

Even when it comes to hearing God, there are multiple ways and reasons that this took place in Scripture. The best way to describe this is that there are four audible voices of God. Or four streams through which the audio of His audible voice is streamed into our lives.

UNDERSTANDING THE VOICE OF GOD

When people say that God has spoken to them, it's possible He has not spoken to them at all, because they have not actually heard His voice. I know many would argue with this, calling it semantics, but we need to understand this on a deeper level. God can communicate with us in nonverbal ways just as well as we humans can communicate with each other. But to hear the voice of God is to audibly hear the voice of God, and nothing short of it. However, many equate the inner dealings and promptings of God to God "speaking to their spirit." The only problem with this is that when we say this, we miss out on the many benefits of God's inner dealings and promptings and what they really mean. The reality is that when our spiritual senses are active, they are engaged with the spiritual world even if we are not fully aware of it.

It is the interactions that our spiritual senses undergo with God that people often equate to inward promptings, impressions, or what they call intuition. This is, in fact, God communicating with us, but it's not with His voice.

Many categorize promptings and impressions as the voice of God due to their lack of exploration of supernatural realities. God has more than a mouth. He is a person and He has created an entire world—a world of worlds—for us to interact with Him, so much so that ultimately His world invades our world.

Understanding this activation of our spiritual senses would bring a lot of clarity to the dreams and visions we experience that lack interpretation. The reality is that there is a lot of spiritual activity that goes on in our lives that happens only because our spiritual man has been awakened by the Spirit of God and by our faith in Jesus (Ephesians 2:1–6). This means that every dream and vision does not need an interpretation. Or better put, they are the interpretation in some instances. They come into our lives simply to let us know that our spiritual senses are active. And because of it, we are able to start noticing and sensing the activity of the spiritual world, which is active and alive around us all the time. Yes, when we are born again, our spirits come alive. We can then both see and enter the Kingdom of God. The entrance into this super-natural dimension often begins with activity that we sense, then our ability to see clearly, and lastly entrance into that world.

What's my point? Many are struggling in an attempt to interpret God's dealings in their lives because they believe the voice of God must be decoded. But it doesn't need to be. Yes, there are some nonverbal ways God communicates with us, but His voice is His voice.

If we are not careful, we will do what everyone who fails to embrace the supernatural essence of the Scriptures does. We will make things that are not symbolic in nature seem symbolic, metaphoric, and parabolic in their existence, which is not true of the voice of God.

To imply that the voice of God in our lives is relayed merely through the construct of our thoughts, an experience of a dream, or any other valid supernatural phenomenon is to imply that God does not literally speak. And yet He does. God does communicate to us in abstract ways, but the reality is that God's actual voice is not heard in abstract ways where interpretation is required to understand it. The voice of God is clear. There's no need to interpret it. The misunderstanding comes when God utilizes our spiritual senses for nonverbal communication in the same way that our spiritual senses are active to discern the spiritual world around us. This means there are times when our spiritual senses are active, but the things we are experiencing are happening more to show us the reality

of God's world than they are being utilized to communicate a divine message from God.

Every time we have a dream, see a vision, see angels,
feel an impression, get a prompting in our spirits, etc.,
does not mean that we need interpretation for what God
is saying. Only experience over time will help us discern
the difference. We need to accept that these types of encounters are connected to a more in-depth reality than
the exercising of merely one of our spiritual senses: hearing. We have been invited to enter God's Kingdom and
experience the realities of His world. This involves more
than God merely speaking to us.

THE AUDIBLE VOICE OF GOD

The audible voice of God is an absolute scriptural
phenomenon. It is literally the experience of someone
hearing God audibly talk to them. It is not something
that happens in our mind, or merely in our sleep. It is a
real experience. Technically, it didn't happen to individuals in Scripture as often as they saw visions or dreamed
dreams. However, the audible voice of God or of angels
was experienced quite frequently in visions and dreams.

Think about it this way. If you were trying to build
a relationship with someone, you would only go so far
by speaking with them over the phone. There's a certain
bond that will grow in a relationship only from the
things that both individuals experience together. There-

fore, most of the time, when an individual communicated plainly with God, it was in a vision. On rare occasions, the voice of God would be heard coming down from heaven without that individual encountering God in any measure outside of His voice.

This happened in Daniel 4, where a voice spoke from heaven. It happened in John 12, and it happened in 1 Samuel 3, just to name a few. Even in my own life it has happened only a couple of times. Every other time I've referenced that I've heard the voice of God, it has been about God speaking in my spirit, which is completely different from hearing a voice outside of me.

My father had an experience of hearing the voice of God. He told me that when he heard it, it was so powerful that it was as if the voice physically shook him. On the contrary, when I heard the voice of God, it was as if it spoke from within me, but also as a whisper in my ear. The differences between what my father encountered and what I encountered are both scriptural.

There are four audible voices of God and they are streamed into our lives through:

The voice of His visitation (1 Samuel 2:4, 6, 8, 10)

The voice that falls from heaven (Daniel 4:31 and John 12:28)

The still small voice (1 Kings 19:12)

Thus says the Lord and thus says the Holy Ghost (Acts 21:11)

I'll start with the voice of His visitation because it is the easiest to understand, whether you believe in spiritual things or not. The voice of His visitation simply means that we hear God speaking to us because He's actually there. This is what happened to Samuel in 1 Samuel 2. Samuel heard God so clearly that he thought it was Eli calling for him. The Scripture clearly shows that the Lord came and stood in the room where Samuel was sleeping when He called Samuel's name. Samuel did not see Him, but the Scripture is clear that the Lord was standing there (1 Samuel 3:10), which is why I call it the voice of His visitation.

The voice that falls from heaven is different from the voice of His visitation. In Scripture, it meant that people heard God speaking, and though His omnipresence was on the earth, His manifest presence was not. This means that God was in heaven and spoke from there, but He opened a spiritual dimension in the earth so that His voice could be heard in the earth as if He were physically there.

The same is true of the still small voice of God. I know the difference because I've heard it before. The only difference between the still small voice and the voice that falls from heaven is in the tone. In other words, the still small voice is more like a whisper from God versus God speaking out loud.

The final phenomenon of God's voice is the "thus says the Lord." This voice is audible because you hear it through someone speaking the phrase. "Thus says the

Lord" is an old English phrase. It lives on today because people have adopted it as prophetic vocabulary. However, "thus says the Lord" is not something that was said in scriptural times to preface a prophetic word. In fact, whenever we read someone saying "thus says the Lord" in Scripture, it was rarely because they were bearing a message from the Lord, but rather the Lord Himself was speaking through their mouth at that very moment. This is one reason 2 Peter 1 says that the spirit of Christ was speaking out of the prophets. When a true "thus says the Lord" moment takes place, even the prophet himself did not know what he was saying until after he had said it, which is one reason I believe they had scribes.

In the times that I have witnessed this, I have found it easy to tell the difference between the individual speaking and when God took over and began speaking through the individual almost as if that person was unconscious of what was taking place while God was speaking. The very atmosphere in the room changes. Even the individual's voice changes. And there is a palpable presence of God that feels as if Jesus Himself is standing there talking with you. It's nothing short of miraculous.

SUMMING IT ALL UP

Scripture is very specific about what level individuals are engaging just one of their spiritual senses—it depends on what level we are accessing the spiritual dimension that determines how engaged we are in the encounter.

Hearing the voice of God is no different from any of our other spiritual senses. Although God does communicate with us nonverbally through various ways, and our spiritual senses are being engaged in the moment, there are times when what we are experiencing isn't meant for communication but for encounter. In other words, there are times where we find ourselves trying to decode and interpret spiritual happenings in our lives that we should be approaching differently altogether.

God's primary way of speaking to us regarding direction—what's right or wrong—is through His Word, not His voice. There is nothing that God will say to us that conflicts with what He has already said. The problem is that if we don't know what God has already said through His Word, there is a 100 percent chance that we will think God is talking to us when He is not. God has instructed us to make the reality of His Kingdom our primary pursuit, not hearing His voice. This means that there are times when we are trying to make sense out of what God is saying when we should be sharpening our spiritual senses instead. Yes, God will speak to us, but most of the time it takes place in the context of Kingdom reality. This is why God spoke predominately through the seer's dimension.

Understanding how to navigate the supernatural comes in layers. There are levels to this reality. It's one thing to prophesy, see visions, and have your eyes open in the Spirit, but it's another thing to mature in it and manifest it in ways that greatly impact the world we live in. The reality is that one of the highest places of supernatural activity is a civilized, intelligent, and very sophisticated state of reality; when you start dealing with principalities, powers, and rulers in ways that potentially influence how entire cities and nations are governed.

Remember, all of the previous realities are not demonic in nature. Don't ever forget that principalities, powers, dominions, might, and every name that is named were created in Christ first (Colossians 1). The reality is that there's a hierarchy in the spirit world that plays a huge part in how our civil life is governed. So much so that for every natural city, for every natural region, for every natural country, for every nation represented, there's a spiritual nation, a spiritual city, etc. This is why the Bible talks about a new Jerusalem, just as there was in Daniel 10 a spiritual Persia—a country that the spiritual hierarchy was set up in—over the natural Persia. This was discovered when Daniel was praying and there was a principality hindering his prayers. My point is that there are extremely sophisticated spiritual beings, both divine and demonic, that work toward its government being the primary influence in the earth in various territories. However, they must partner with individuals who understand how to interact with their world in order to establish their spiritual influence in our natural world. On the divine side, there is God and the angels that work for Him. On the demonic side, there is the devil and the demons that work for him.

God is always looking for men and women who will advance His Kingdom in the earth. He wants His world to come in our world as it is in heaven (Matthew 6:10). His world is always around us, within arm's reach. His Kingdom is at hand, near, and readily accessible. However, seeing and entering that reality requires us to allow the Spirit of God to birth us into the supernatural dimension. And once we are born, we must then continue to seek the development of our newfound spiritual senses so that we can mature, grow, and become able to interact in that invisible world. You will see an increase in your spiritual sight and the activation of your spiritual senses as you dig deeper into knowing God.

CHAPTER 9

NINE WAYS TO INCREASE YOUR SPIRITUAL SIGHT

You've learned about your spiritual sight; now let's deal with how to increase its operation in your life.

1. OBSERVATION

The first way to develop your spiritual sight is to observe. You must have a certain level of expectancy and a certain level of awareness that what you see is not what you get. There is more to this world than what meets the eye. There is activity going on behind the scenes right now, always. The key is to live with that awareness. And then, if you start looking to see, you will see. This is what God taught Jeremiah. God asked Jeremiah, "What do you see?" Once Jeremiah answered, God answered back and said, "You've seen correctly" (Jeremiah 1:12 NIV). When God asked Jeremiah what he saw, it was an invitation to look. Afterward, the vision did not appear to Jeremiah until after he had looked. And it was only after Jeremiah reported what he had seen that another vision followed the first. In other words, his sight increased when God allowed him to see more.

This is what observation is all about. You are not going to see if you don't look.

2. FOCUS

The next key in developing your spiritual sight is to begin to start focusing on what you're noticing. This is what happened to Peter. He had a vision in Acts 10, and then he told his testimony of the vision in Acts 11, which is where he gave the secret of what sharpened his sight. Let's look at the portion of the text that shows this reality, and please take time to read Acts 10 and 11 soon.

But Peter rehearsed the matter from the beginning, and expounded it by order unto them, saying, I was in the city of Joppa praying: and in a trance I saw a vision, A certain vessel descend, as it had been a great sheet, let down from heaven by four corners; and it came even to me: Upon the which when I had fastened mine eyes, I considered, and saw fourfooted beasts of the earth, and wild beasts, and creep-

ing things, and fowls of the air. And I heard a voice saying unto me, Arise, Peter; slay and eat. But I said, Not so, Lord: for nothing common or unclean hath at any time entered into my mouth. But the voice answered me again from heaven, What God hath cleansed, that call not thou common. And this was done three times: and all were drawn up again into heaven. And, behold, immediately there were three men already come unto the house where I was, sent from Caesarea unto me. (Acts 11:4–11)

Notice, it was not until Peter said that he fastened his eyes, that the vision opened more to him. This is true focus. This is where many people miss out on supernatural encounters, because the reality is that many supernatural encounters do not open in a blatant or boisterous way.

Moses is another great example of this secret. He's in the wilderness and notices a bush burning. The only problem is that it was typical for Moses to see a burning bush, because he was in the desert. What caught Moses' attention was that the bush was *not being consumed* by the fire. Then the Scripture goes on to say that Moses turned aside to see the flame in the bush. This means he gave it his full attention. Had it not been for this, Moses would never have understood that the reason the bush was not being consumed by fire was because the angel of the Lord was in the flame.

Did you notice the progression? Moses first noticed the fire, then noticed the fire was not consuming the bush, and lastly, he noticed that the angel of the Lord was in the bush after he had given the moment his focus (Exodus 3:2–4).

The same thing happened to Peter. Everything began with him seeing something floating down from heaven toward him. The Scripture says he saw it, focused on it, and then pondered on it. What followed then is that the experience evolved out of merely seeing something into the audible voice of God speaking to him in a trance. That is the power of developing your sight. You must focus on what you're noticing no matter how insignificant it seems.

When I first began seeing in the Spirit, I would see sparkles, flashes, and various lights. I didn't start seeing on the level I wanted to right away, but the more I engaged that dimension, the more I began to see. You may have experienced the same thing and thought your mind was just playing tricks on you. Nothing's wrong with your eyes. Start paying attention, and you will see more.

3. FAITH

Jesus said in the book of John that "if thou wouldest believe, thou shouldest see the glory of God" (11:40). He did not say that you *shall* see, but that you *should* see. This takes on a whole new dynamic. It is stating that seeing is our right—it should not be denied to us.

Faith is significant to spiritual sight in ways beyond what we previously covered from 2 Corinthians 4:17 to

5:7. Let's go deeper as we examine its reality. Faith comes by hearing, and hearing, by the Word of God (Romans 10:17). Here, we're going to focus only on the emphasis of "hearing." It's significant because it is scientifically proven that the part of the brain that gives your hearing its functionality is the same part of your brain that gives your imagination functionality. This part of your brain is called the pineal gland. Maybe this is yet another reason why sight is referred to as the "eyes of your understanding" in Ephesians 1:18.

The reality is that our spirit forms images in our mind around whatever we allow through the gates of our ears. Therefore, I often teach that faith is not faith until after you have imagined what you are believing for. You must see yourself already where you're trying to go. You must see yourself already healed. Imagine how you're going to walk when you get out of the wheelchair. Imagine how you're going to feel when you stop going to chemotherapy. Use your imagination. It increases your faith and it also sharpens your sight, especially when you're reading the Bible.

When you read the Bible, see yourself in the den with Daniel and the lions. See yourself walking through the Red Sea with Moses. See how the whales and sharks and sea turtles look through the walls of the water that were parted. Use your imagination. You'll be surprised at the things you will encounter in God just by integrating your imagination in the way you read the Scriptures and allow the Scriptures to come alive in your life. God can utilize your imagination while it is engaged in what the Scriptures do speak, and cause your spiritual sight to be sharpened. The least that will happen is that your faith will be strengthened. And that alone should never be shunned.

We need to know it's okay to really believe God.

It's okay to believe that greater things are going to take place.

It's okay to believe that though it seems there's no way, God will make a way out of no way.

It's okay to believe that God can do the impossible.

It's okay to hope for tomorrow.

It's okay to believe for something no one else will understand or figure out how God did it.

Faith never makes sense anyway. So we might as well use our imagination. God wants us to see it in the supernatural before we see it in the earth. He wants us to see it in the Spirit before other people see it in our lives. That's how you sharpen your sight. Faith sharpens sight.

4. EMBRACING THE MIND OF GOD

"The god of this world hath blinded the minds" (2 Corinthians 4:4). I love the fact that this Scripture speaks of the blindness of our minds, because in doing so, it exposes where the spiritual blindness originates, which is in the mind. Any area where there is ignorance pertaining to God's word is a blindside for you.

When we neglect spending time in God's Word, it's like using your peripheral vision in the spirit. There are so many who wait on a prophecy or the next sermon from their favorite preacher, not understanding that this enables spiritual blindness in their lives.

I love prophetic ministry, but we must get into the Word of God, and know the mind of God concerning what His will is if we are going to develop strong spiritual sensitivity. The Word of God is required in sharpening your spiritual sight and removing the blinders from your mind. You see, your perspective and your perception coincide. So if my perspective is off, if my mentality is off, there's a blinder on my mind. When there's something wrong with our ability to perceive spiritual things and to have insight into a matter, it's usually because we don't know the mind of God from the Word of God.

The Word of God and the Spirit coincide. There is no spirituality without Scripture. Any presentation of the supernatural that is not laced in the Word of God cannot and should not be trusted. Likewise, God doesn't even trust us to engage certain dimensions of the supernatural if He sees we are ignorant of His Word, which is our only safety in the spiritual dimension.

We can come into a new trust to steward various things in the Spirit when God sees that we have His mind and heart, which is found in His word. In fact, God wants to trust us with greater things in the supernatural, which is what 1 Corinthians 2:11–16 is speaking of.

Do you see what the Scripture is insinuating? Having the mind of God is so powerful that God will start taking your instructions into consideration. Smith Wigglesworth must have understood this. He was known for saying, "If God don't move, I'll move God." I believe he said this because he understood the power of knowing the mind of God. I also believe he knew the mind of God, because He believed the Word of God. And just in case you've never heard of Smith Wigglesworth, you need to know that it does not get too much more credible than Smith Wigglesworth pertaining to the Christian faith in the twentieth century. He was a man who raised over forty people from the dead. If you go to a local library today, you can pull up an article on him that will show you one newspaper reporting that he raised somebody from the dead out of a coffin. The man even raised people from the dead out of the ICU, in hospitals. The man raised his own wife from the dead. Smith was known, and is still known today, as a man who had a certain mentality about the supernatural power of God that he refused to waver from. This is the strength of knowing the mind of God.

Your sight will only be as strong as your perspective, and your mentality will only be as strong as your spiritual sight, which will only be strong as you embrace the Word and the mind of God. Do you want to see? Do you want to move in the supernatural? You've got to get into the mind of God, through the Word of God. There is absolutely no way around this principle.

5. PRAYER

Matthew 26:41 tells us to "watch and pray." Notice Jesus didn't say "pray and watch"; He said "watch and pray." Because not only is your sight strengthened through prayer; your sight is what prioritizes your prayer life. If we do not pay attention to what God shows us in prayer, then we will not know how to strategize our prayers to become more effective. So when you're praying, there needs to be a dialogue, not a monologue. You can't be doing all the talking. You must watch and pray.

More specifically, Jesus was teaching prayer in the context of the prophetic anointing by mentioning both watching and praying, because watching is a seer's dimension. It's an invitation to utilize the prophetic and the seer's dimension to become more effective in the way we pray. The more you pray, the more God is going to open your sight. The more you see, the more effective you're going to be in prayer.

6. BEING STIRRED

"The Lord stirred up the spirit of Cyrus king of Persia..." (Ezra 1:1). The word *stirred* in the Hebraic tongue means to "open the eyes." This is key, because although God stirred the spirit of Cyrus, there are times when He expects us to stir ourselves. Timothy was told to stir the gift within himself (2 Timothy 1:6–7). God also told Isaiah that He looks for me that will stir themselves to seek Him (see Isaiah 64:7).

Regardless of the reason or the context, our sight and our sensitivity to spiritual things are often determined by how stirred our spirit is. Therefore, there are times that God will allow things to agitate you. He'll allow moments and maybe even seasons of frustrations, because there is something He's trying to get you to consider so that He can show you something. His aim is never to discourage you, but to give you insight into a situation. Sometimes you're in a situation that's uncomfortable and you think you're waiting on a miracle from God. Instead, God is saying that the miracle is already within you.

This brings us back to the story of the widow in 2 Kings 4. When Elisha addressed the widow, he showed her that although she needed a miracle, she also needed to do inventory, which is why he asked her, "What is in your house?" The widow was so blessed after that particular insight that it caused her to go from almost losing her home to opening a warehouse. She went and borrowed vessels in order to get out of debt, which means God turned her debt into equity.

There are times God wants you to know that everything you need is already in your house. God will stir your spirit. He will allow frustrating seasons, because frustration is the beginning of revelation. You'll know your hard season is ending by the level of frustration you develop for where you are. It is in these moments that God intends your spirit to be so stirred that He can show you key and critical insights that will help you transition so that you don't become stuck in an old season. This is why God stirs our spirits. He knows that the revelation and insight we gain in the stirring are critical to the time only in which they are relevant.

This is what harvest time is all about. Let me explain. "Harvest time" has become a key phrase that many believers reference to identify with the blessing of God. We utilize the metaphor to communicate the blessing because, agriculturally, harvest represented a return on investment. Harvest time meant that we would see new results for our efforts and real productivity in our work. However, we often don't acknowledge that harvest time required a certain seizing of the time in order to reap the benefits. Jesus even mentioned the importance of discerning the timing of the harvest in John 4.

In harvest time, a farmer works the hardest, more than when he was planting seeds. Harvest time always means that the farmer will need to put in extra hours, because he knows he has only a certain amount of time to get to the wheat before wild animals get to it, before the locusts get to it, before the palmer worms get to it, or before it begins to rot.

This is what God does: He stirs your spirit, He challenges you, He allows you to go through frustrations because He's trying to open your eyes. When God sends a harvest, the time of harvest could potentially be the most frustrating, the most stretching, the most challenging time in your life because you have only a moment of time to get to the harvest before the harvest rots.

If you want to see in the Spirit, you have to be able to deal with frustration and allow the frustration to stir. If you do, you will get to a place where you will understand there is no existence of a problem, except where there is the existence of a solution. You see, before you were aware that there was a problem, you were comfortable in the problem. So when God allows you to be in times of deep frustration, you must understand that it's because the level you were formerly comfortable in now is a problem for you. Problems do not come into existence until their solutions are premade. When you've been in a place too long, God will stir your spirit, so that you can see there is something greater for you on the horizon.

7. CARRYING A BURDEN

A burden was whatever was strapped onto oxen for the transport of a heavy load. A burden, at its most basic spiritually, represents the concerns of God being processed through the emotions of man. It's most active in the case of injustice or a people who lack a relationship with God. A burden manifests when things happening in the earth bother you because they bother the heart of God more. The reality is that God will entrust a level of sight only to people who are concerned with what He's concerned with. The burden of the Lord becomes the sight of the Lord. You will begin to see with His eyes. You'll see things from His perspective. You won't look at the world through the lens of CNN. And because of this, your perspective won't be swayed by popular opinion. You'll always see from the sight of God. You'll always see things from a positioning, from a vantage point of how God sees things. You can always measure an individual's maturity in the prophetic by how much of a burden you detect in their sight.

This is what happened in Habakkuk 2:1, when he stood on his watch. His sight was different because his vantage point was different. The secret here is that what we studied earlier in Habakkuk 2:1 began in Habakkuk 1:1 when we read of "the burden which Habakkuk the prophet did see." Here, the sight that Habakkuk had begun with was a burden. Likewise, when we become sensitive to what's dear to God's heart, it only means that God is trying to open our eyes and give us insight into His Kingdom. This goes hand in hand with prayer. Those who carry the burden of the Lord are those given to prayer and intercession.

If God can trust you to be in prayer, then supernatural things will occur. You might be praying, and all of a sudden, you'll be able to see what's happening in China before it happens in China. You'll be able to see things before they take place. You may even begin to see a crisis before it happens so that things can be averted in prayer.

Seeing in the Spirit is not about showing off a gift.

God wants to put His burden on you so that He can open your eyes to see what He wants to show you and things that are coming in the future. The way we engage our sight could potentially impact matters of great significance in the earth. This is why God filters a level of our sight though His burden.

8. ENCOUNTERS

There are great benefits in seeking God and having encounters with His Spirit. It's often in an encounter with God that your eyes are opened.

We know this now, but how do we get there? I'll show you a secret. Whenever you're in a place of prayer, and you're allowing yourself to be in the presence of God, don't let the end of your prayer be the point of breakthrough. What I mean by this is that you should not get up from your prayer position as soon as you become aware of the presence of God, or when you know your prayer was heard, or maybe even when you know your prayer was answered.

The secret is that if you wait long enough, if you make it beyond the tears, if you make it more than just a good worship session, something deeper will take place. If you stay in the presence of the Lord, if you stay long enough and wait for Him, He'll open your eyes and show you something more. And don't we long for more of God?

When all the exhilaration of prayer is gone, when

there are no more emotions and no more tears to cry, wait. Stay in His presence with your mind focused on Jesus only, and give Him the invitation to show you what He wants to show you.

If you don't see anything the first day, the first couple of months, the first couple of years, keep waiting. My story is that I waited for years, and over time God gradually began helping me to see more clearly in the Spirit.

9. LIVING UNDER AN OPEN HEAVEN

There are many Scriptures that link open heavens and spiritual sight. Here are a few: John 1:50–51; Matthew 3:16; Acts 7:55. Living under an open heaven is living full of the Holy Ghost, as we've previously discussed. You can also see the correlation of this in two of three of the previous scriptural references. Being full of the Spirit and the heavens opening are simultaneous. You can't be full of the Spirit and the heavens not be open. If you are full of the Spirit, the heavens open.

Remember, it was when the heavens opened that the Spirit of God descended on Jesus in Matthew 3. Furthermore, it was when Steven was full of the Spirit that he looked in the Spirit, saw the heavens opened, and saw the glory of God. The supernatural is all about living a life full of the Holy Spirit, and when you're living a life full of the Holy Spirit, you're living under an open heaven. This is was also true of Ezekiel.

The Scriptures say that it was when the heavens open that he saw visions of God and the Spirit entered him (Ezekiel 1:1).

Whether the heavens open after the Holy Spirit comes or the Holy Spirit comes after the heavens open is of little importance. The important thing is that we acknowledge the correlation of this reality and how it links to the seer's dimension, granting us entrance into visions and encounters.

GOING DEEPER IN THE SUPERNATURAL

I want to take a minute to talk about the power of God, and biblical truths concerning miracles, signs, wonders, and other things of that nature. It represents a totally different side of the supernatural, the side that gets everyone's attention. However, it thrives off the strength of everything we've learned up till now.

The supernatural is more than miracles, signs, and wonders. It is the reality of God and His desire to establish His Kingdom among men. Embracing the power of God in your life is the next appropriate step. Are you ready to embrace all that God has for you? He's waiting for your "Yes!"

CHAPTER 10

POWER AND AUTHORITY

The significance of the *power of God* is paramount. We cannot represent God or His Kingdom without it. The reality is that visions and encounters consist of how we see, enter, and operate in the Kingdom of God. The power of God, on the other hand, is how we demonstrate the Kingdom of God in the lives of people who have not yet seen or entered His Kingdom. The power of God bears witness about His Kingdom to those on the outside.

A HISTORY OF THE POWER OF GOD

When I experienced Jesus for the first time, I knew that the supernatural was key for those around me who didn't think He was real. From that moment on, I knew I needed to carry the power of God, and I knew it would get people's attention.

I have seen tumors dissolve. I have seen cancer healed. I have seen blinded eyes open. I have seen deaf people hear. I have seen people get up out of wheelchairs and walk again and people no longer in need of their oxygen tanks. I've even seen God dissolve metal implants and replace the metal with healthy new bone. This list goes on. God has used me in many miracles, all of which have been medically verified. There's obviously quite a lot I've learned over the last eighteen years in ministry concerning God's power. But honestly, I have not always placed as much emphasis on teaching it for a reason. The reality is that there is a difference between the presence of God and the power of God, as I mentioned in Chapter 1. And if you never learn to distinguish between the two, you will miss the most important thing to be pursued in your life: the presence of God.

I learned this from Pastor Benny Hinn. Around thirteen years ago, Pastor Benny began hosting trainings for ministry conferences around the United States. I traveled to as many as possible. You'd most likely see me on a lot of the video footage at those conferences because my friends and I attended so often that the staff began sitting us in the pulpit with all the other more well-known preachers, although we were not known at the time. And then at one of these conferences Pastor Benny showed me why I needed to distinguish the presence from the power of God. It's an extremely important lesson to learn in ministry. If you don't learn it, you will think you're seeking God, but really you only want His power for yourself.

This is why I teach the power of God only to those who have first fallen in love with His presence. Although miracles, signs, and wonders are extremely important, to *know* and use miracles is not what it is to *know* God.

I want to first establish a foundation in this truth. Afterward, I will go into some detail concerning what the Lord has taught me about the difference between power and authority.

PRESENCE VERSUS POWER

As I've just said, there is a difference between God's presence and God's power. God is Spirit (John 4). Therefore, the Holy Spirit is not an "it" and you don't "catch the Holy Ghost," rather you are *filled* with the Holy Ghost. He is a person. He is the very Spirit of Jesus. The reason this is important is because it is not until you begin treating the Holy Spirit like a person that you'll see your relationship with God begin to develop.

There is a key in understanding the difference between the presence and the power of God: the presence of God is God being present. He is ever present. He is everywhere at the same time. He is never absent. This is the key distinction between the power and the presence of God, so pay close attention. If the presence of God is never absent, it means that God is with us whether we feel, experience, or ever become aware of that reality. It is consistent. The presence of God never leaves you. On the other hand, the power of God is *felt*. If it is not experienced; it is not present. Therefore, the presence of God is understood in the *existence of who God is*, but the power of God is understood in the *experience of what God can perform*.

"Without faith, it is impossible to please him: for he that cometh to God must believe that he is, and that he is a rewarder" (Hebrews 11:6). Here, Hebrews is explaining more about the mystery of God's presence than most ever give credit to. Consider this. The Scripture is saying that when you come to God, you must believe He is. In other words, there is emphasis on His existence alone. He is. Period. I Am that I Am, He said of Himself (Exodus 3:14). He is already here, He always has been in existence, and no one can get rid of Him. Therefore, just because you don't feel, experience, or become aware of God's nearness doesn't mean He's not God. He is.

Understanding God's presence is understanding that He is always with you whether you are aware of Him or not. There are many times you may become aware of His presence, but it is never because He was absent before you became aware. When you're happy, He's there. When you're sad or when you're hurt, He's there. When you're in pain, He's there. God is always there. He never leaves us. However, our faith in this truth is the only way we can begin experiencing this reality. When we come to

God, we must believe that He is. That's where an awareness of His presence begins—with faith, not feelings.

On the contrary, God's power is more easily detected. Our experience of God's power can be likened to the tides of the ocean. It comes in waves through all the ups and downs. At times, we could be experiencing His power more, and at other times we could be experiencing His power less. His power comes in degrees, in measures. His power is administered in multiple ways. Acts 1:8 says that we "shall receive power, after that the Holy Ghost is come upon you." According to this, you have access to all the power you will ever need. God's power resides in you. However, if you are not seeking a lifestyle of being filled with and led by the Spirit of God, you are not accessing that power of God in the way that God originally designed.

The key is not to seek the power, but the person and presence of God, because there is an illegal way to access the power of God, which I'll explain further. This is where spiritual authority comes into play. Understanding the proper spiritual authority is like understanding the proper guidelines and boundaries of moving in the Spirit. The attempt to move in the supernatural without these guidelines can be detrimental.

PRIORITIZING THE PRESENCE OF GOD

It is the Spirit of God that allows us to become aware of the presence of God. It's also the Spirit of God that administers the power of God. Understanding this helps us view Acts 1:8 through a different lens. The reality is that many seek the power of God, but have no desire for the presence of God. However, for the power of God to be released in our lives, the presence of God is required. This is the reason the text says we receive power after we receive the Spirit.

The reality of His presence is totally different from the reality of His power. Therefore, once the Spirit of God enters our lives, it is up to us to prioritize seeking the reality of God's presence over seeking the reality of His power. If we do not, it is very possible to begin accessing the power of God illegally. When this takes place, the power of God will still accomplish what the power of God is designed to accomplish. But when Jesus looks at it, He classifies this as a work of iniquity (Matthew 7).

Our motive for pursuing God must be to know Him, and not to pursue Him for what He can do for us or through us. He wants a relationship with us, which is the agenda of the supernatural.

The legal way to manifest the power of God is both through the infilling of the Spirit and by the leading of the Holy Spirit. However, the technology and the potency of God's power are so advanced that there are ways that wicked men manage to avoid this. Even Moses understood this when he struck the rock in the wilderness and caused a miracle to take place in which water began to flow out of the rock for the refreshment of the Israelites, who were passing through.

The children of Israel were in the wilderness and needed water. Moses prayed and God answered, instructing him to strike a rock and water would flow out for the Israelites to drink. Moses struck the rock, water came out, everyone drank the water, and the people were happy. Well, one day they needed water again. However, this time God instructed Moses not to strike the rock, but to talk to the rock instead and then water would flow out. The only problem was, Moses had the bright idea to strike the rock again because he knew it would work, and it did. When Moses struck the rock, although God had instructed him to do something else, water flowed from the rock. This is a great example of accessing the power of God illegally. Moses didn't get away with it. God called him out for it.

Knowing and understanding things like this can better help you identify the difference between God's authority and God's power. It's just as important as understanding God's presence and God's power.

THE ORIGIN OF SPIRITUAL AUTHORITY

There's an understanding of authority that comes only from examining God's original intent when He made man. Therefore, it is no coincidence that the root word of "authority" is the word *author*, because it points back to the beginning of things.

Considering this, I believe the simplest way to explain

authority is to explain it as the trust that God originally extended toward mankind to share in His dominion. This is what happened to Adam and Eve. Scripture says that God let them, or better said, gave them permission to have dominion.

The proper protocol in which authority is extended is through a relationship of trust. It is then maintained by its level of stewardship or the way the individual who is trusted with that authority adequately manages what's within the confines of the authority granted. The reality is that power is a Kingdom commodity. Therefore, you really can't deal with power and avoid authority.

Those who prove to lack pursuit for the presence of God or resist spiritual authority are also those who will prove to abuse the technologies through which God designed His power to be expressed. When this takes place, an individual can seemingly be doing the work of God and yet working iniquity, as I have previously pointed out in Matthew 7.

WHAT IS AUTHORITY AND HOW DO BELIEVERS ACCESS IT?

Authority is the right we have as children of God to live a life of victory, free from demonic bondage. It is also our legal right to exercise God's power to implement the realities of that victory in our everyday lives.

Because of this, I think it's best to begin explaining

authority in context of our conflict with demonic powers so that those being introduced to the concept have a solid foundation. This is not evolving into a book on deliverance, but we must touch on some truths concerning spiritual authority in the context of our victory over the enemy. There's no way to avoid it.

Authority in every believer's life was established by the finished work of Jesus Christ on the cross. We have full victory over every demon in hell by the shed blood of Jesus Christ, and the following are great examples of that reality:

"Having disarmed the powers and authorities, he [Jesus] made a public spectacle of them, triumphing over them by the cross" (Colossians 2:15 NIV).

"For this purpose the Son of God was manifested, that He might destroy the works of the devil" (1 John 3:8).

"Through death he [Jesus] might destroy him that had the power of death" (Hebrews 2:14).

"And this is the victory that overcometh the world, even our faith" (1 John 5:4).

These are just a few of the many Scriptures that confirm that we have authority over the devil. But remember, authority is not just authority over the devil. Authority is your right and your permission to experience the promises of God. However, if this authority is being challenged by hell, God has various systems of rank through which that rebellion is properly dealt with for our safety. This is one of the reasons why the power of God becomes necessary. Power is often the reinforcement of the promise, and this is where power and authority meet. For example, just because I own a gun doesn't give me the license to use it however I wish.

There are measures of authority. There are also measures of authority we step into gradually as we are trusted to steward that authority. On the one hand, all believers have authority over the devil. We all have authority over the power of hell that seeks to resist the promises of God in our lives for healing, prosperity, deliverance, and freedom. We all have authority to win in life. We have permission to succeed, and we have permission to be victorious. On the other hand, there are measures of authority that are actualized in our lives by how we walk with God, not by works but by grace. It is only as we walk with God that we are trusted to steward greater measures of authority to enforce our God-given right in the earth.

Let me show you how this works. The truth is, we don't have to fight a devil that's already been beaten. We must look at Scripture that speaks about the finished work of Jesus Christ to understand the principle of communicating spiritual authority. Matthew 12:29 says, "Or else how can one enter into a strong man's house, and spoil his goods, except he first bind the strong man? and then he will spoil his house." This is in context of the Pharisees questioning Jesus for having so much success in casting out devils. Owing to His highly successful deliverance ministry, Jesus is accused by the Pharisees of casting out devils because they say He possesses the power of a demon Himself. But Jesus explains His power by associating a captain among evil spirits to what He classifies as a strong man. Furthermore, in this Scripture, He begins to explain that He is not the strong man, but rather the *stronger* man who goes into a strong man's house and binds him with the intent of gathering his goods.

Jesus did this often during His life on earth, but He did this once and for all when He went to the cross. At the cross, Jesus was the stronger man that bound the strong man (Colossians 2:15). The strong man is bound. You see, if you are in the world, the devil is the god of the world, but when you come into the Kingdom, the devil is only the prince of the air.

So when you move in the authority that is already granted in the finished work of Christ, then the enemy is *already* bound. What the devil tries to do is keep you ignorant of what belongs to you or distracts you from pursing the presence of God so that he can overstep that authority. This is really where spiritual warfare begins. It's not about picking fights with the devil because the devil is already defeated. It's not so much about fighting devils as it is growing into a place of understanding of what belongs to us first and foremost. Then, as that takes place, we come into a trusted walk with the Lord in which we learn to utilize the authority granted to us to enforce what belongs to us. There is no prince, principality, or power that has not been made subject to Jesus, the King of Kings. He is that stronger man that binds the strong man. Period.

CHAPTER 11

FIVE WAYS TO MEASURE AUTHENTIC SPIRITUAL AUTHORITY

1. REVELATION

Revelation is one of the first things that reveals the increase of authority. You can tell how much authority an individual is walking in by the level of revelation they're walking in. In other words, your authority in God is based on your level in the Word. This is because the enemy's only leverage in overstepping God-given authority is ignorance. More specifically, to pinpoint your sphere of authority is to examine what you see when you read the Scriptures. What stands out to you the most? What lens are you looking through when you read the Scriptures? When you read the Bible, is salvation all you see? Are blessings all you see? Is the supernatural or dynamics of the spiritual realm all you see? What revelation are you getting? What insights stands out to you most? This is what I mean when I say your measure of authority is based on your level of scriptural intake.

Let's look at what Scripture shows of this reality. In Matthew, Jesus asks Peter, "Who do you say that I am?" (16:15 NKJV). After Peter responds with the correct answer, Jesus reveals the authority that revelation accesses, informing Peter that he has answered the question correctly because the answer was revealed to him (vv. 16–17). Jesus proceeds to tell Peter that He is giving him keys which are symbolic of the authority he will walk in. This is the power of revelation. Peter's revelation of who Jesus is awarded him a set of keys to the Kingdom, which houses the authority to bind, loose, and prevail against the gates of hell. It's simple: no revelation, no keys.

Your Word level must match your spiritual level. Why? Because the Word of God is the law of God. This is what Proverbs 16:10 speaks of: "The lips of a king speak as an oracle, and his mouth does not betray justice" (NIV). When a king speaks, it is law. This is the law that Romans 8:2 speaks of. There are laws in the Spirit. The Scriptures also teach that the enemy is an accuser and Jesus is our advocate. An accuser is a prosecuting attorney, and an advocate is a defense attorney. This means that the spiritual battle is often more legal than anything else. Therefore, are you often overcome by examining and enforcing the legalities? How do you enforce them?

By knowing the Word and following the leading of the Spirit. In other words, just as if you were in legal trouble and needed an attorney representing you in the natural, you need the same in the Spirit. Why? Because you don't know all the laws. When you allow the Spirit of God to teach you the Word of God, then you learn the legalities of the Spirit. When you learn the legalities of the Spirit, which is the Word of God, when anything that is opposite of the promise of God presents itself in your life, you can take authority over it.

So, the way you increase your authority is by increasing your Word level. You must have a Word level or you won't have anything to move on and the Holy Spirit won't have anything to administrate when you need the power of God to be active in your life. If you haven't already, start reading your Bible daily!

2. STEWARDSHIP

The second way you can measure your growth in spiritual authority is by stewardship and faithfulness. More simply: It's doing right with what you have. God looks at our faithfulness in small areas to determine our promotion. For example, the proper order of progression in life is not to believe that life gets better only after you get everything you desire. Life gets better when you want it to get better. A good life is not dependent on where you live, what you drive, or how much money is in your account. Of course, we can have those things, especially if we first seek the Kingdom, according to Matthew 6:33–34. The problem is that when we seek to obtain things that we are not willing to properly manage, it is often a sign that seeking the Kingdom was never our motive in the beginning. For example, if I desire to have a mansion, but can't keep my current apartment clean, my level of stewardship demonstrates to God that I might not be ready to own a mansion. The point is that authority is more of a responsibility than it is a desire to rule.

Furthermore, stewardship is not only taking care of the little you have, but also taking care of what belongs to other people. Stewardship was also the context in which dominion was defined to Adam and Eve. God did not just give them dominion, but He gave them dominion in the context of them taking what they had, making it fruitful, and multiplying it (Genesis 1:28). One way to be trusted with more of your own is to be faithful with what others already have, according to Luke 16:12. This is where serving comes into play. God gives no one authority who does not have a servant's heart. However, there are many who desire authority or even set themselves in authority but avoid the way of the servant. If you really want authority in God, you must become a servant. You must find someone who has a vision in life or ministry greater than your vision, and serve them and the vision. There is no legitimate promotion into power, authority, or influence apart from servitude. Any other promotion is of the devil.

The way you increase your authority is by doing right with what you have. It's about being faithful with small things, faithful with what belongs to others, and believe it or not, Luke 16 also mentions the importance of being faithful in finances. The way God elevates and promotes people into power is through seeing them faithful over small things. You must embrace a spirit of greatness before you see greatness. You must embrace a spirit of excellence before you see excellence.

3. RELATIONSHIP

The third way to measure growth in authority is through relationship. I love this principle of measuring our growth in the authority we have in Christ because it allows me to expound more on the truths from the previous chapter concerning the origin of authority. Remember in Matthew 20:20–23 when the mother of the sons of Zebedee asked Jesus to allow her sons to sit at the right and the left side of Jesus? They understood authority in a way we often overlook. The right hand of power is the highest level of authority that can be conferred by a ruler. Furthermore, this level of authority is referenced by how closely positioned the individual is to the one who rules, which is at the right hand.

In the spiritual realm, power is in proximity. Just as our reputations can become more favorable or unfavorable by our associations in the natural, so is there power in proximity in the Spirit. Anyone who stands in the presence of God will take on the attributes of God. This is what we see happening to both Gabriel the angel and Elijah the prophet. Gabriel was given great authority by God to deliver a message, so much so that he caused Zacharias to go mute when he did not believe the report that Gabriel came to give from heaven. Furthermore, Gabriel's statement that revealed the basis of his authority to do what he did was that he stood in the presence of God (Luke 1:19). Proximity.

The same is true of Elijah, who was granted authority by God to speak to King Ahab and have power to cause it not to rain on the earth for a three-year period. When the king asked Elijah who he was, the king was basically asking him who granted him the authority to come stand before him. Elijah's response was that he stood in the presence of God. Therefore, in both the New Testament and the Old Testament you see two messengers, one prophetic and the other angelic, referencing the power and the authority granted to them by God to proximity.

However, the proximity of the right-hand position was only partially why the authority was granted. The position of the right hand signifies the relational dynamic of the one closest to the ruler, which is why Jesus sits at the right hand of the Majesty.

The reality is that we don't grow in authority in our attempt at taking charge, or our pursuit of promotion. We grow in authority by drawing closer to God.

The closer you get to God, the more you will walk in spiritual authority.

4. MEASURE OF OFFICE

Ephesians 4:11 states, "And He Himself gave some to be apostles, some prophets, some evangelists, and some pastors and teachers" (NKJV). As believers, we all have authority. There is a basic authority in every believer's life based upon the finished works of Jesus on the cross. You must know the Word to know your authority. Let's first briefly understand our authority in Jesus and then briefly distinguish it from the authority He placed on various offices of ministry.

The sufferings of Jesus released certain benefits that His death did not. His blood released certain benefits that His sufferings did not; even His cross released certain benefits. There are benefits in His resurrection, His ascension, His constant intercession, and His immanent return. What does His blood yield to us? What does His suffering yield to us? They didn't put a crown of thorns on Jesus for no reason. There was an inheritance released in that. Everything Jesus did and everything He is yet doing yields us a right and authority to experience the best of God. We cannot honor His death and His resurrection only.

Jesus did not merely rise from the dead, and that was the end. There was and is a measure of authority in His ascension and in His priesthood. He is a priest forever after the order of Melchizedek. And according to Romans 8:29, He is conducting His priesthood in constant intercession. That alone is powerful.

Jesus is not in heaven just waiting to return to earth, sitting at the right hand of God. In Acts 7:55, Stephen saw Him standing, Mark 16:20 says He works with His apostles, and again Romans 8 says He's making intercession. This is the inheritance of His ascension. Jesus ascended into a priesthood in which He is the faithful priest spoken of in 1 Samuel 2, who serves God forever.

There is a measure of authority in this alone that is delegated only to chosen officers, which we call the fivefold ministry. It's an authority to serve as an officer, which is quite different from the broad context of authority we all have as believers. It's a priestly authority, and Scripture says priests minister pertaining to the house of God. This means that within the leadership structure of the Church, everyone does not have the same authority as delegated officers of God within God's house.

We must separate the two because Scripture says that He has made us kings and priests. The fivefold ministry gifts are priestly offices that have authority in the household of God to oversee the growth and grooming of the people of God. In other words, although we all have authority, we all need leadership. Everyone can't be in charge in God's Church, which is why Jesus gave gifts to men in Ephesians 4:11. The word *gifts* there is not the

Greek word *charisma*, as found in 1 Corinthians 12, but the word *doma* which is defined as an "office." Jesus delegated His authority among five priestly offices to govern the household of God. Therefore, a measure of authority can be determined only by the measure of an individual's office. However, it's not just the office alone that determines the measure of authority, but also an individual's commitment and faithfulness in that office. This is key because there are many who feel that embracing the title of a fivefold ministry office automatically grants them authority because they understand there is a measure of authority in the office. However, I reiterate, our office is not the only thing that determines our authority.

An individual can be an apostle or a prophet but have less authority than the Church's janitor because they have lost their prayer lives, or are not in the Word anymore. The authority of an individual's office is not about their title or about their position in the Church. It's about their willingness to serve God faithfully and keep first things first, which is seeking His Kingdom and His righteousness.

5. CHARACTER

Character is the fifth and final key I'd like to cover in measuring authentic spiritual authority. Character is simply the quality of your personal development. It is the maturity of your spirit man. The more you grow in your spirit, the more you become like God. Therefore, we must commit to growth.

Remember when Elijah was hiding in a cave? It was there that God told Elijah to anoint Elisha as a prophet in his room or sphere (1 Kings 19:16). The key here is that Elisha received a double portion of Elijah's spirit, not his anointing. The significance of this is that the Scripture was referencing Elijah's human spirit with emphasis on the quality and integrity of Elijah's personality. This was the prerequisite of Elisha entering Elijah's space of authority.

Likewise, when God sees growth in our character, He opens a greater measure and sphere of influence. This is how your authority increases. Your character not only is what gives you access to exercising influence, but also will determine the longevity in which you occupy whatever sphere or authority granted to you by God.

CHAPTER 12

THE SCIENCE OF POWER

In the last conversation that Jesus had with His disciples before leaving the earth, He promised us power: "But you shall receive power, after that the Holy Ghost is come upon you" (Acts 1:8). However, it seems the power that Jesus promised is more so embraced by charismatics and Pentecostals than any other community of believers, although it is promised to us all. Furthermore, the promise of power is often referenced from this verse among Pentecostals. The only problem is it is parallel with the last chapters of the Gospels and does not stand alone. Which means you will not understand the power of God if you study only Acts 1:8. The reason is because the conversation of power is synoptic, a term explaining the unique differences in the Gospels, which consists of the first four books of the New Testament. It simply means that each gospel highlighted a different detail of something in the life of Jesus although it was expounding on the same story.

For example, if Jesus was healing a man, one gospel may have emphasized how the man came to Jesus while another may have emphasized how Jesus came to the man. Same story, different emphasis. The same is true of Jesus' teachings. We see this specifically with the parable of the sower, recorded in Matthew, Mark, and Luke. However, we see different aspects of the same truth in each writing. When dealing with the Gospels, you must parallel every mention of a specific story or parable. The truth must be connected like dots. The mysteries are like pieces of a puzzle.

The same is true of what Jesus taught His disciples concerning the power of the Holy Ghost. It is synoptic. Therefore, although the promise of power is mentioned in Acts 1:8, it cannot be captured in this verse alone. When Jesus promised the power of the Holy Ghost to His disciples, He was extensive in detailing what they were to expect. But the details of everything the power of God would represent are not featured in just one Scripture. We must compare multiple Scriptures of the New Testament that reference the conversation that Jesus had with His disciples concerning the power they would receive.

There are five books of the New Testament that feature the promise that Jesus gave His disciples after His resurrection concerning the power they would receive. Therefore, if we are going to understand the power that

Jesus promised in its full extent, we must compare what all five books feature from the exact same conversation that took place. We will discover that each book highlights a different facet of the power of God. We must bring it all together to gain a unique understanding, because the power of God is indeed multidimensional and multifaceted.

UNDERSTANDING THE POWER OF GOD

The final conversation that Jesus had with the disciples before His ascension is featured in Luke 24, Matthew 28, John 20, Mark 16, and Acts 1. Furthermore, power is mentioned in three different contexts all within the same conversation.

The power of God is extensive and intrinsically understood. The following references will help you embrace this concept as you move along:

Power in Three Contexts

Acts 1—Power received within
Mark 16—Power is with you (atmospherically)
Luke 24—Power comes on your life as opposed to within

We can see that there is a complexity to power, not because it's hard to understand, but because there is a science to how power operates. The power of God is a multifaceted phenomenon. I believe there's a reason that the Gospel of Matthew introduces the conversation of power in the context of "all power" (28:18). Power is dimensional. This is also probably why every gospel after Matthew mentions power in a different context. It's because there's much to learn about the power of God. In fact, I want to show you a Scripture that mentions four types of power in one verse. Here are two different Greek words for power: *dunamis* and *exousia*. *Dunamis* deals with explosive power of God, while *exousisa* deals with authority. When you read the word *power* in the New Testament, it could be referring to one or the other. In fact, the word *power* in English has at least three basic Greek words that represent it. The third is the Greek word *kratos*, which literally means "manifested dominion."

Furthermore, there are more words in the New Testament that detail the power of God. More specifically, this one verse in Ephesians blows my mind concerning the understanding that can be gained pertaining to the power of God: "And what is the exceeding greatness of His power toward us who believe, according to the working of His mighty power" (1:19 NKJV). Here, there are four Greek words that define four different aspects of God's power: *dunamis*, *kratos*, *ischus*, and *energeo*. The word *ischus* deals with force and might. The word *energeo* deals with efficiency, which is the one we need to understand most from the text to embrace the science of how power operates. So let's examine the text to see how it reads in the original language: "the exceeding greatness of His explosive power *(dunamis)* toward us who believe, according to the *efficiency* (working/*energeo*) of His mighty force *(ischus)* manifested dominion (power/*kratos*)."

THE SCIENCE OF POWER SIMPLIFIED

It's only as we remember that power is dimensional that we begin to understand what Ephesians 1:18 is conveying, especially in the context of efficiency. Basically, there must be an inner working of power within us that is synergizing with an external active power of God and produces the miraculous in and through our lives.

This is what efficiency is all about. For example, if I have a thousand-wattage device, I can't expect to charge it with a hundred-watt power surge because the power would then not be sufficient. Things work the same way in the Spirit. Remember, at minimum, we are dealing with power that we receive within (Acts 1:8), power that is with us wherever we go atmospherically (Mark 16:17), and power that comes on us (Luke 24:49). At any given moment, any of the previous avenues of power could be at work. However, they must work together efficiently.

This is the science of power. There are so many gifts, technologies, and administrations that efficiently connect us to how the power of God may be moving within us, on us, through us, for us, or around us in the atmosphere.

There are some basic things you can consider in helping you broaden your perspective of God's power, which will cause you to better understand what I'm communicating. I want to deal with four of them here.

FOUR WAYS TO BROADEN OUR UNDERSTANDING OF POWER

1. Stretching Your Paradigm of Power

The way you stretch your paradigm of power is to go beyond the basics of what many generically teach concerning the power of God. A great place to start is to gain an understanding of how power is multidimensional, by the example recorded in Jesus' post-resurrection conversation in Mark's gospel. Mark 16:17 clearly says that signs will follow believers. It goes on to give a list of things that will be evident in the life of believers. This is key because a sign is a demonstration of God's power. Therefore, Mark 16:17 is detailing multiple dimensions of power to help us begin understanding the broad extent of God's power.

The basic power dimensions mentioned in Mark 16:17–18 are healing, speaking in tongues, authority over demons, and protection. However, power is mentioned in the context of prophecy and miracles in

Matthew 7. Power is also mentioned in the context of wealth in Deuteronomy 8:18. Lastly, it is mentioned in the context of promotion, leadership, and influence in the Book of Psalms and the Book of Romans.

The more we search the Scriptures concerning God's power, the more we discover an expansion upon this concept. Another way to embrace the vast extent of God's power is to think in the context of all power, not just spiritual power (Matthew 28:18).

2. Consider Natural Power

In Matthew 28:18, when Jesus mentioned power, He did so in the context of all power in both heaven and earth, not just spiritual power. This will also prove to give us a wider context in comprehending God's sovereign ability. The reality is that the supernatural power of God can be superimposed over every natural power, whether it be hydro, solar, electrical, or even atomic. Think about it. When Moses parted the Red Sea, that was hydropower. When the sun stood still, that was solar power. Think about when the three Hebrew boys withstood the fiery flames. All weaponry including atomic weapons are powered by fire, which is the very thing that God answers with.

The power of God can literally alter the laws of physics. The Scripture is literal when it tells us there is nothing impossible with God. Supernatural power also often utilizes natural power as a foundation from which to launch in divine exploits. Therefore, the natural theories of power can be paralleled to scriptural truths, metaphorically, to aid us in understanding how spiritual power functions as well.

3. The Difference Between Signs, Wonders, and Miracles

The next thing you should understand is that there is a difference between signs, wonders, and miracles. They each represent a different aspect of God's power.

I've been learning this phenomenon for the last eighteen years, and it never ceases to amaze me how God continues to build on this in my life. The difference between miracles, signs, and wonders is that miracles prove to be provisional of a need, signs tend to be directional, providing navigational or supporting with evidence, and finally, wonders leave us in awe of God. Wonders come to wow us. Signs come to direct or assist us, and miracles come to meet a need. It's just that simple.

When the Lord taught me this, I began noticing that Scripture is very specific in its choice of classifying the displays of God's power throughout history. The Bible intentionally calls a sign a sign, a wonder a wonder, and a miracle a miracle.

I invite you to consider this truth when reading about God's power. You'll then more readily discover the purpose behind God's power being revealed throughout various biblical stories.

4. Comparing the Synoptic Gospels' Descriptions of Power

The final key brings us back to where we began. If you're going to understand what Matthew 28:18 means when Jesus talks about what all power is inclusive of, you must begin by referencing it synoptically in Mark, Luke, and Acts. And remember, although the Book of Acts is not a gospel, the first chapter of it features the final conversation Jesus had with His disciples after His resurrection.

Referencing All Power Synoptically

Mark 16:17—Power follows us
Luke 24:49—Power clothes
Acts 1:8—Power is received within

Power is on us, in us, and around us. This is what I mean by the science of power. There are so many dynamics that could be at work at any given moment when the power of God is active. These are things we should learn in order to become proper custodians of God's supernatural power. It's a mystery and yet God does not complicate the matter as it pertains to our faith. God only expects us to depend on Him as a child and expect Him to honor His word. In other words, the only requirement to be a recipient of God's power is that you believe. However, if you ever run into problems and hindrances in an attempt to demonstrate God's power, it's only because becoming an authorized dealer of God's power has separate criteria we must be trained in.

Let me explain. The reach of God's power is endless, yes. There is nothing God cannot do and there is nothing we cannot do when our faith is in Him. There is nowhere that our minds can reach that God's power cannot reach. However, this is our foundation. The reality is that you can receive God's power in your life according to Acts 1:8, and yet not know how to cause that same power to begin to be active on your life (Luke 24:49) and around your life (Mark 16:17). It's one thing to understand and embrace God's power; it's a completely different story to know how to operate in it. Read on, and I'll show you how.

CHAPTER 13

POWER TECHNOLOGIES, HEALING ADMINISTRATIONS, AND MIRACLE MOVEMENTS

As they pertain to God's power, healing and deliverance are foundational and fundamental in understanding the various administrations of how the power is dispersed. Through examining this, we discover biblical tools and spiritual technologies by which the power of God is more efficiently activated. This is what I want to deal with in detail throughout this chapter. I want you to know how to see the power of God in operation in your life. I call this the technology of power and the administration of miracles.

In fact, there are many biblical phrases that describe the release of power and the avenues through which it is demonstrated. When you see any of the following from now on in Scripture, I want you to think in terms of these realities existing as spiritual technologies that service the display of God's ability through our lives more effectively. These terms are:

The Ministry of Spirit (Galatians 3:5)

The Demonstration of Spirit and Power (1 Corinthians 2:4)

The Acts of God (Psalm 103:7–9)

The Gifts of the Spirit (1 Corinthians 12:7)

The Weapons of our Warfare (2 Corinthians 10:4)

The previous is a brief example of why I say that healing and deliverance become the basic standard of measure because of how the power of God is not limited to them. This is merely one reason I often teach that power is dimensional. Furthermore, not only is power dimensional, but at this point, we are expanding on that thought in a rather unique manner. I reiterate, our focus in this chapter is expounding on the different ways God's power is administered.

For example, sometimes miracles happen with more of our involvement and other times with less. This is no different than when Jesus would merely speak a word, and other times when Jesus would lay His hands on people in need. In addition to this, there are also varying appropriations of God's power. I'll continue to explain this reality in the context of the miraculous.

I've discovered that miracles are gradual at times, and sometimes they are immediate. Sometimes miracles have more impact in the lives of onlookers and sometimes miracles impact various individuals on a personal level without anyone else even being aware of them. This is what I mean by varying appropriations of the miraculous—different demonstrations of power have varying strength levels.

Jesus said that we would do the works that He did and even greater works, in John 14:12. There is a such a thing as greater works. We must embrace the fact that some miracles are just plain greater although everything God does is great. However, we must also understand that the miracles are *not* greater because they require more power, but rather because they make more impact. Check out the following examples of greater works:

Special Miracles (Acts 19:11)
Notable Miracles (Acts 4:16)
Infallible Proofs (Acts 1:3)
Creative Miracles (Matthew 15:30–31)
Strange Acts (Luke 5:26)

These examples all show when the miraculous is out of the norm. They are proof of how signs and wonders often reach beyond the parameters of the occasional healing and deliverance. There is a dimension called greater works, and believe it or not, this is the foundation from which the Lord taught me concerning what I classify as advanced technologies of the Spirit. The logic behind this is simple. For example, I do not expect my car to travel with the proficiency of a jet because it does not have the tech for that. The same is true in the supernatural. There are certain dimensions of power that utilize various advanced operations of the Spirit to become active in our lives. There are levels of power that are not released in the anointing of oil or the laying on of hands. Certain things that even Jesus and the apostles did show evidence of another spiritual technology at work than the customary tools and utilities of healing.

For example, Peter did not have an online course on how to heal people with their shadow. Paul did not go to the school of prayer cloths. There is no doctrine of angels that oversees healing pools. And if you read the Gospels carefully, you'd discover that the pool of Bethesda was only one of the healing pools mentioned in them.

There are healing movements of the past and recent history that been accompanied by more than a gift of healing or miracles. The Lord has shown me this reality. Over the years, I have become aware of if I'm moving in a gift of the spirit, or a resident healing anointing. I can discern if there is an atmosphere of healing or if power is flowing according to an individual's faith. The Scriptures are specific to the previous realities. However, it's hard to decipher what is being communicated through such occurrences without insight into the supernatural.

I'm completely aware that many may feel this is too technical. After all, the technicalities are the responsibility of a professional, not the average person. I don't get paid to do what my mechanic, my lawyer, or my accountant does. They are the professionals so I let them do the work, and they explain to me what I need to know to cooperate with their plan of work. Although this may be mind blowing, let me be the professional here. I can promise you that a couple failed attempts at pulling someone out of a wheelchair or raising the dead and you wouldn't think twice before reading this book again.

There are levels to all of this. And this is what we discover that Jesus suggested, if you combine Matthew 7 and 10. Although Matthew 7 shows mighty works in a negative connotation, Matthew 10 shows mighty works in the positive, communicating to us that it was, in fact, the desire of Jesus to perform mighty works in the text, but the people did not have the faith for it. In both texts, there is a mention of mighty works, not to mention the other texts in which the mighty works of Jesus are mentioned. We should understand that the mighty works have a correlation to greater works. It's a consistent theme in the Gospels. It's like tomato, tomahto.

Therefore, the texts suggest that some works are mightier than others. More specifically, it is the mentioning of mighty works in the context of the laying on of hands that gives us insight into the reality of power technologies. In the text, Jesus is classifying what works are mighty and what works are not when He talks about laying hands on individuals to receive healing as being the only administration he could operate in for healing after verifying that no mighty works took place. The reality is that if no mighty works took place but Jesus laid on hands, it means that the laying on of hands is not a mighty work. Therefore, the text reveals that the laying on of hands is not an advanced technology in the Spirit. In fact, Hebrews 6:1–5 confirms that it is indeed an elementary principle.

So what are these advanced technologies of the supernatural power of God? I'm going to explain this within three basic truths to provide context. Let's examine the technology of power and various administrations for healing in the context of the following three truths: power and authority over all sickness and devils, resurrection power, and the ministry of Jesus Christ.

THREE BASIC POWER POINTS

Power and Authority over All Sickness and Devils

I want to get straight to the point. Mark 3 teaches that we have been given power to heal the sick and cast out devils. In fact, Luke 9 and 10 teach that we have been given authority over all devils and sickness. This is important because the Scripture does not say that we have power and authority over some devils. It does not say that we can cast out a lying spirit, but cannot cast out a jezebel spirit. No. It says we have power and authority over *all* devils. Furthermore, the Scripture also does not say that we have authority and power over just some sicknesses. It does not say that we can heal back pains but cannot heal cancer. No. It says we have authority and power over all sicknesses.

It is important that we embrace the previous truths because of the simple fact that if Jesus needed to demonstrate the power of God in order to authenticate His message, how much more do we? It was Jesus who promised that we would do the very same works that He did, according to John 14:12. And if we are truly going to flow in the miraculous, we have to get to the place where we embrace this kind of faith. We must get to the place where we realize that there was not one sickness that Jesus did not heal and not one demon that Jesus refused to cast out of the individuals who came to Him. Therefore, the reality is that the works that we are called to duplicate are the works in which all are delivered and all are healed.

I understand that many reading this book will most likely need a jump start in their faith concerning this, and that is exactly what this chapter is prepared to do. I'm going to jump into talking about faith for raising the dead and healing for the sick. Faith for resurrection is where faith begins, according to Romans 10. It is not the pinnacle of our faith but rather the foundation of our faith. If we can believe that God can raise the dead, we can believe Him for anything.

Faith for Raising the Dead and Healing the Sick

First off, I want to clarify that the reason I teach about raising the dead is because the Bible teaches about raising the dead. In fact, there are nine primary instances recorded in Scripture of the dead being raised. There are others that are often overlooked that we will examine later in this chapter, but for now, check out the following list of the nine primary resurrections and review it for yourself:

Nine Resurrections

Elijah and the Widow of Zarephath's son (1 Kings 17:17–24)
Elisha and the Shunamite's son (2 Kings 4:36)
Elisha's bones raise a man from the dead (2 Kings 13:21)
Jesus and the widow's son at Nain (Luke 7:13–15)
Jesus and Jairus' daughter (Matthew 9:25)
Jesus and Lazarus (John 11:43)
Jesus raised from the dead (Matthew 28:5–7)
Peter and Tabitha (Acts 9:36–42)
Paul and Eutychus (Acts 20:9–12)

In addition to the previous nine, there is a possibility of Paul being raised from the dead found in Acts 14:19–20, but we cannot necessarily count this one because the Scriptures do not clearly verify it. Now with that in mind, the question is, why is this ministry of resurrection important? Let's look at 1 Corinthians 11:30 for the answer to this question. According to 1 Corinthians 11:29–32, it is possible that individuals are sick although God does not desire anyone to be sick. It is also possible according to the text that individuals die before their time. However, it's not God's will that we are sick, and it's not His will that we die early. Not to mention, there's an enemy out there who has no other agenda but to steal, kill, and destroy. With this in mind, we should cultivate a fresh fervor in seeing the resurrection power of God in manifestation. In fact, let's now begin with the healing ministry as a foundation in understanding how often God wants to manifest this type of resurrection power in our lives.

Healing on Every Level

When we read Matthew 4:24 and see Jesus healing every sickness and disease, there is a powerful revelation that becomes easy for us to overlook if we fail to probe deeper into the Scripture. I personally was prompted to take a deeper look, and I discovered that the words "sickness" and "disease" are from two different Greek words. In fact, if you study the words closely, you will discover that one has more emphasis on external physical ailments and the other on internal ailments. Jesus heals all, whether it be a common cold or a terminal illness.

The revelation is simple and yet profound that God has healing for the total man no matter what the sickness or the disease is. Exodus 15:26 teaches that He is the Lord God that heals us. Malachi 4:2 says He rises with healing in His wings. Psalm 103:2 reassures that He heals all of our diseases. Isaiah 53:5 says that by His stripes we are healed. The list of healing Scriptures goes on. However, Isaiah 53:5 is another healing Scripture that brings confirmation to Matthew 4:24 in the very fact that it says that by His stripes we are healed.

The stripes are significant because it is believed that Jesus received thirty-nine stripes, which is key because there are believed to be only thirty-nine root causes for every known disease. Simply amazing. You can always go back over the teaching with your Bible at any point. However, now that you know that there is healing for every sickness and every disease, let's shed light on some of the specific illnesses that the Scriptures mention being healed, and let's understand them.

We often read how Jesus healed the palsy, the maim, the halted, etc.; and although it sounds good, we do not know what those words mean. Therefore, I have taken the time to define some of the healings of Jesus so that the next time you read them, it will have more impact on your faith.

Take the time to review some of Jesus' most notable healings along with the definition of the particular illnesses that we may often overlook. Afterward, take the time to locate specific instances in the Scripture in which the following illnesses were healed:

The Blind and Deaf are self-explanatory.
The Lame represents the crippled.
The Halted and Withered represents the disabled.
The Palsy represents the paralyzed.

The Maim represents those with missing body parts.

The Lunatic are likened to those with autism or schizophrenia, or who are severely bipolar.

The Lepers were those with skin disease and are also likened to those with terminal illnesses.

DIFFERENT ADMINISTRATIONS OF HEALING

According to 1 Corinthians 12:3–5, there are different administrations of how the Lord moves, which means that there are various methodologies in how God's power is dispersed. So this means that just as the gifts of healing represent only one of nine gifts of the Spirit, there are also other administrations in which healing could take place without the gifts of healing being in operation. This teaching is important because in addition to embracing faith for the miraculous, one of the most important keys in flowing in the miraculous for healing and deliverance, other than having a genuine compassion for the lost, is to understand the different administrations of healing. There is no one method that heals everyone.

Jesus showed us that the key to the miraculous in His ministry was based on Him moving however the Father wanted Him to move, according to John 5:19. Check out the following references for examples of Jesus operating in various administrations of healing, which is key to understanding what He meant in John 5:19:

He sent the word. (Matthew 8:8–13)

He gave an instruction. (Luke 17:14)

He anointed with oil. (Mark 6:13)

He preached and healing power was present. (Luke 5:17)

He laid hands on them. (Mark 16:18)

People touched the hem of His garment. (Matthew 14:35–36)

People would be healed as they were slain in the Spirit before Him. (Mark 3:10–11)

The previous are great illustrations of what I mean by different administrations of healing. However, there are other examples of this layered in Scriptures that I believe we have overlooked. I want to expound on a couple briefly because there is a great wisdom that can be unlocked concerning flowing in the miraculous in just being able to discern these various administrations.

THE LAYING ON OF HANDS

And these signs shall follow them that believe; In my name shall they cast out devils; they shall speak with new tongues; They shall take up serpents; and if they drink any deadly thing, it shall not hurt them; they shall lay hands on the sick, and they shall recover.

Mark 16:17–18

Many read this passage and in faith go to apply the Word of God in the area of healing, only to eventually end up frustrated because they do not understand the administration of healing that is promised to be in operation. In fact, I have discovered that only those who persistently stepped out in faith, on the basis of this Scripture, are the ones who have, through experience, discovered the revelation of the text, which is that the administration of healing promised to be in operation in Mark 16 is that of a recovery and not that of an instantaneous miracle. The difference is that a recovery is gradual in nature, but a miracle of healing, in most cases, is immediate. For example, when Peter healed the man who was impotent from birth, the Scripture says that the man's anklebones immediately received strength, according to Acts 3:7. This is why when Peter is giving testimony to the healing in Acts 4:22, he calls the healing a miracle and not a recovery.

THE WORKING OF MIRACLES AND THE GIFT OF FAITH

Although the working of miracles is one way that healing can be administered, there is yet another gift of the Spirit that can administer healing as well. It is called the gift of faith. It operates differently than the working of miracles. When the working of miracles comes, there is usually some type of participation supernaturally in our lives in the area in which the healing is needed. This is why is it called the working of miracles. If we do not work at it, we do not see the miracle. This is why Peter pulled the man to his feet in Acts 3:7. He was getting the man to work his faith in the area in which he needed the miracle. The gift of faith is, however, a little different and a little more aggressive in nature.

You see, the working of miracles may help someone to their feet, but the gift of faith will tell an individual to stand up on their own. It requires a little less assistance. It knows what it knows, and sometimes seems to move aggressively within an individual when in operation.

You see, the working of miracles was in operation when Jesus formed mud and placed it on the blind man's eyes in John 9:6–7, but the gift of faith was in operation when Jesus told the paralyzed man to take up his own bed and walk in John 5:8. These are two different administrations. Does this make you take a closer look at the gifts of the Spirit or what?

And there is yet another administration of healing that I believe we often overlook that I want to deal with here. I know I didn't go into great detail concerning the working of miracles and the gift of faith, but there are other books you can read for that. My job is to get you to recognize the various administrations, but in the meantime I suggest that you read what Smith Wigglesworth, Lester Sumrall, and Kenneth E. Hagin wrote about the gifts of the Spirit for more clarity.

THE GIFTS OF HEALING

The gifts of healing are an administration of healing that is different from the working of miracles and the gift of faith, in that it is exclusive to healing. However, what is often less obvious about this administration is that the word *gift* is plural in 1 Corinthians 12. This means that out of all nine gifts of the Spirit, the gifts of healing are the only manifestation of the Spirit that has multiple gifts locked into one.

This means that although there are nine gifts of the Spirit, there are many gifts of healing. What I mean by this is that each gift of healing operates in an area of specialty to cure a specific ailment. For example, just as there is a difference between an eye doctor, an ear doctor, or a cardiologist, there are various areas of endowments in healing.

This mystery is that when the gifts of healing are in operation, there are individuals who see more results in certain sicknesses being healed depending on what gift of healing is dominant in their ministries. I've studied the generals of the faith of times past and discovered this to be true in their lives as well as in my own. Personally, I've seen more results in tumors being dissolved and various body pains ceasing than any other healing, although I have seen deaf ears opened, blind eyes opened, and other notable miracles as well.

Have you ever wondered why you go to a service and people with pain are healed but not the people in wheelchairs? Well, it just depends on what gift of healing is dominant in the ministry that God is using at the time. There are even times where the deaf, the blind, and the paralyzed can get healed and yet others would probably leave with terminal illnesses remaining in their bodies.

We have to understand that when this administration of healing is in operation, people do not leave a church service sick because God chose not to heal them. The truth is that the gifts of healing are designed only to function within a certain capacity. The problem is that we as believers have to be willing to press beyond our comfort zone in the way we flow in the miraculous in order to stretch our capacity to see more of God's power in demonstration.

It is easy to see a couple of results and get comfortable in a place that was meant only to be the training grounds of a greater place. The good news is, for those who are hungry for more, there is a greater administration of healing, of which the gifts of the Spirit are a bridge into. In fact, I believe that this next administration is the greatest administration of healing in which all can be healed, and I am going to explain why.

HEALING EN MASSE

The gifts of the Spirit are a sort of training wheels pertaining to demonstrating the power of God. They are designed to train us to a point in which the Spirit of God can manifest whatever gift He would like to, as He wills (1 Corinthians 12:11). This is why it is important to recognize the administration that the Lord is moving in, so that as He moves, we can yield to it, and as a result, healing can manifest for everyone.

I like to call this healing *en masse* or mass healing. And the reason that I believe it is the greatest administration of healing is because it takes place only in the very presence of the Lord Jesus, in which He Himself does the work. Only Jesus healed everyone and only He can. However, I believe that we can so yield to His presence that He initiates this administration through us.

Many have begun to refer to this as "presence-healing." In fact, both Pastor Benny Hinn and my spiritual father, Apostle Guillermo Maldonado, operate in this administration quite often, in which they simply enter the Lord's presence through worship and allow the Lord Himself to do the healing. It is a powerful dimension that I believe we have yet to see the fullness of, but I believe the more we depend on Jesus and enter His presence, the more He will move with us in this capacity.

HEALING FOR ALL

Almost everywhere in Scripture where the people brought the sick to Jesus, the Bible declares that every one of them were healed (Acts 10:38). In fact, the Bible speaks of how Jesus healed everyone just as much as it speaks of various individuals' personal accounts and testimonies of healing.

For example, the Scriptures mention Jesus healing every sick person that came to Him at least ten times in the Book of Matthew alone, which is only one of four gospels. In comparison to this, there are only thirty-one individual testimonies of healing when including all four gospels.

Healing for All

Matthew 4:23–24
Matthew 8:16
Matthew 9:35
Matthew 10:1
Matthew 12:15
Matthew 14:14
Matthew 14:35–36
Matthew 15:30
Matthew 19:2
Matthew 21:14

I took my liberty in making the previous list available to you concerning Jesus healing all in the Book of Matthew for a reason. I'm afraid that when we refuse to acknowledge overarching healing and we make mention only of the cases in which Jesus healed specific individuals, we cause the healing power of God to seem as if healing is exclusive to only certain individuals. This could not be further from the truth. In fact, there is a reason that certain individuals' healings are mentioned in the Scripture.

There are only two reasons that the Scripture emphasizes certain healings of various individuals. The first gives us more insight in the administrations of healing operative in the life of Jesus, and the second leads to my closing point of this chapter. The first reason that Jesus healed certain sickness more predominately is due to the gifts of healing that were in operation at the time, because remember, the gifts of healing and working of miracles both operate in areas of specifics. Whenever a multitude came to Jesus, the Scriptures either state that all were healed or mention only the people with various types of illnesses that were healed.

From experience, I believe this took place because faith is a key element in seeing an advanced technology of power come into operation according to what we previously examined of Matthew 10. I reiterate, this is also true of experience, and it's also what we see if we pay close attention to the gospel stories of how the multitudes came to Jesus.

I noticed that after Jesus would operate in the gifts of healing for the multitudes, something would take place. The Scripture taught that the multitudes would go out, spread the word, and then bring more people to Jesus to be healed. Furthermore, I noticed that these were the times in which all would be healed. This is a great example of how the gifts of the Spirit became a bridge into the greater administrations of healing.

The second and only other reason that individual Scriptures emphasize certain healings is because of the cultural significance behind the story of their healing, and not because the healing was exclusive. For example, according to Matthew 14:36, the woman with the issue of blood was not the only one attempting to touch the hem of Jesus' garment. And according to Matthew 10:8, Lazarus was not the only person being raised from the dead (see also John 21:25). Let me briefly expound on the cultural significance of Lazarus being raised from the dead as opposed to all the others who were raised from the dead in those days.

THE LAZARUS EFFECT

The significance of Lazarus being raised from the dead deals with how influential he was in that time. He was wealthy, he had great authority in the region, and everyone knew who he was. Therefore, Lazarus being raised from the dead had a very strong cultural impact to it.

For example, overseas, there are people being raised from the dead all the time, especially in Africa. Therefore, if someone's neighbor died and was raised from the dead, it would not have as much of an impact as raising the president of China from the dead. Do you get the point?

When Lazarus was raised from the dead, it impacted the culture so much that when the religious leaders conspired to kill Jesus, they made plans to kill Lazarus as well. The reason is because the resurrection of Lazarus had so shaken up the region that they knew that even if they killed Jesus, it wouldn't matter if Lazarus was alive. The effect that his testimony would have on the culture would be as if Jesus were still alive. Isn't the thought of this powerful?

IN PURSUIT OF THE SUPERNATURAL

The truth of the matter is that just as healing took place regularly, so did the resurrection of the dead. According to Matthew 10:8, the Lord had clearly given the apostles authority and power to raise the dead in every city that they preached in, which brings me to this point. Maybe the resurrection of the dead had become so common in the ministry of the apostles that by the time we land in Matthew 27:52, in which our Bibles clearly articulate that countless individuals had been resurrected at once, no one had any reason to be afraid. Maybe by that time, they had become so accustomed to witnessing the dead being raised that the possibility of so many individuals being raised from the dead at once was not a shock to them. My question is: What type of world would we live in if it once again became common for the Church to operate in resurrection power, flowing in signs, wonders, and miracles?

We must keep things in this perspective if we are going to understand the power of God. We must always be mindful of the reality that we are dealing with the power that brought the world into existence.

Of course, there's much more I could teach on the supernatural, but the point is not to merely learn it, but to know it through experience. You can find out more about the courses I teach at unquenchedthebook.com. You see, there is no over-the-top when it comes to the supernatural. If we can imagine it, our God can exceed the abundance of all that we can ask or think (Ephesians 3:20). There is nothing that God cannot do, and nothing that we cannot do through Him.

We as Christians should have a Lazarus effect. Our testimonies of God's power should be impacting the world around us in ways in which our lifestyles yield the results that prove the fact that Jesus is still alive. This is what resurrection power is all about! And it's yours. Draw close and lean in to what God has for you today. "And what shall I more say? for the time would fail me to tell..." (Hebrews 11:32). I want to end this book the way Hebrews 11 ends its tale of faith, in pursuit of more. It's time to say yes to the more He has for you!

ABOUT THE AUTHORS

Jonathan Ferguson is first and foremost a family man. He travels extensively and has been featured on several international television stations such as Daystar, TBN, the Word Network, and more. He is sought out for his revelatory teaching/preaching. Jonathan's ministry is marked by the evident demonstration of the supernatural presence and power of God, merging its reality in everyday practical living.

Amanda Ferguson is a wife, mother, speaker, author, and business owner who is passionate about empowering the "total woman." She is the creator of the prestigious Feminine Woman Academy, the top-rated podcaster of *The Amanda Ferguson Show*, and has been featured in media appearances such as "Her Story" on *Joni Table Talk* and her very own documentary created by The Green Room Team on Daystar called *The Amanda Ferguson Story*. She enjoys spending time with her husband, having fashion shows with their three daughters, and vacationing in places with sunny climates and beautiful beaches.